TO HEAR
THE FOREST SING

.

TO HEAR THE FOREST SING

SOME MUSINGS ON THE DIVINE

Margaret Dulaney

LISTEN WELL PUBLISHING

For my mother

Cover and interior design by Brooke Koven
Illustrations by Carolyn Mercatante
Edited by Aina Barten
Copy edited by Hayden Saunier
Cover art by Jane Morton Norton

ISBN 978-0-9986023-0-1

Contents

Pieces of the Puzzle

Confirmation

The writings in this collection are a result of
a quarter of a century of morning walks in the woods with
my dogs,
just under a half a century of literary exploration of the wisdom
of the world religions,
and a lifetime's hunger for God.

Foreword

WHEN MARGARET DULANEY asked me if I would "blurb" her latest book of essays, taken from her spoken word website, "Listen Well," I hesitated. I'm one of the many who were urging her to publish her audio essays as a book. I wanted to hold it in my hand, have the luxury of re-reading, reflecting, rolling that sentence on my tongue again. On the other hand, I make it a practice not to write blurbs for any authors, it's so time-consuming, such responsibility, not to mention hard to write; but even the best-held principles fall by the wayside.

I agreed.

She sent me the manuscript, and I had hardly read three essays when I knew I didn't want to write a blurb: I wanted to write the foreword.

This book is too good to let pass with a phrase: "a book to treasure," or "everyone should have this on their bedside table."

Margaret is a poet and playwright, a storyteller and teacher. "The writer Joan Grant," the first sentence of the first essay begins, "believed that every human being was both teacher and pupil and that at any moment we are instructing someone and learning from someone else...." The instant anyone stops learning, Dulaney continues, he loses the ability to teach, and the human awakening toward enlightenment will falter.

Margaret Dulaney says she's my student. Well, she's a teacher to me, and I think I'm the winner in that exchange, for her soul is so pure, her heart so willing that whenever I am in the dumps I have only to talk to her, or listen to an essay from "Listen Well," to be reminded again how to pick up my feet and place them again on the Higher Path.

There are such individuals living among us, perhaps you know some. They are not saints. They are simply quiet individuals, living quiet lives in out-of-the- way-places, often wise beyond their years, and of a goodness of heart that puts everything into perspective for the rest of us. They don't do social media. Some don't even use cell phones or computers (in this day and age, imagine!). Some don't read the daily news or watch television, or "keep up." Yet these are the ones, I find, who teach me most.

I met Margaret through a family connection and was instantly taken by her gentleness and generosity. She is one of those people whom you can almost hear listening intently to the music of other spheres, even as she's attending to your needs. And that's what I find in this short collection of stories or essays.

Essay: an interesting word.

To essay is to attempt or try; an essay is the result of your effort, and we often think of an essay as dry and as lifeless as the paper that is disintegrating between your impatient fingertips.

But hers run in the tradition of Ralph Waldo Emerson (one of her heroes, as we discover to no one's surprise). They are thoughtful, self-aware, brimming with questioning and curiosity, and the pursuit of the meaning to life.

LUCKY THE READER, then, who plunges into these stories, and I suggest a running dive—waste no time—because, if you are like me, you want to swim long in these waters, float on the twists and currents of her thinking. Once in, you don't want to climb out. But these rivers run deep. You might be able to handle three, even four, essays at a time, but then you need to breathe. Reflect. Reluctantly you climb out, towel off and remove your bathing suit, shivering. If you're like me, you have the sense, fragile as intuition, that somehow you've been changed, though you don't quite know how.

Some things are instantly clear: her use of language and metaphor is a delight. Her verbs leave your heart singing; her phrases make you burst out laughing with joy. She is, "a foul-weather friend, dashing in with extra raingear to save those [she knows] from any discomfort." She speaks of "the hounds of doubt" that "chase down a rising prayer, circle it, and shake the poor thing by its scrawny neck." She talks of "the changeable weather of my mind," of her "Inner Bossy Pants," her lack of confidence, the pterodactyl of despair that drops from the skies without warning and grabs her in its barbed wire claws (Oh, yes, don't we all know that pterodactyl with his 20-foot wingspan?). And always, running throughout, is her sense of humor. In one story, a big dog comes flying at her so joyfully that "it occurred to me that he might have mistaken me for a large squirrel."

A READER ALL her life, Margaret quotes the I Ching, Hafiz, Rudolph Steiner, Swedenborg, Bill Wilson, Ralph Waldo Emerson, George MacDonald—an amazing array. But her own words carry equal weight.

Sometimes you find yourself stopped short by the way she shifts from serious to comic, shaking you like a terrier with a toy. Describing refugees who spend years of heroic struggle in the effort to save their lives and those of their brothers, who walk out of war, find haven in tent-cities, and eventually plod to foreign countries, where they question, finally, the purpose of living, she comments: "People, it seems, do not like being treated like caged hamsters." And then, letting us off the hook of horror: "But then I suspect neither do hamsters." This is followed by her soft, sweet point. "Love, these boys had, love was all around them."

It is a theme that runs throughout the book: love, enlightenment, hope, a sense of purpose to life, the suggestion we are learning over the course of millennia as one by one, like popcorn, we awaken: "pop. . .pop. . . pop . . pop. . pop, pop, pop, pop, pop. . . . One pop, and then another pop, then another and another, pop pop pop pop pop pop pop!!" She draws our attention time and again to "the remarkably intricate design that weaves all of our needs into such a fine pattern" that if we could unwind the thread the complexity of coincidences would blow our minds.

The idea that there IS meaning, a Presence watching over us, her confidence that somehow we are progressing even if reaching grade 3 takes 300 years, her deep, compulsive curiosity "about the divine workings behind the material world," her conviction that progress is found in deep listening, slowing down—no hurry, stop, just look, and become aware of the inner Shepherd leading us—all this is right up my alley.

Story after story is thought-provoking, like her nephew who believed after a car accident that he was talking to God.

"What are we supposed to do with life?" he asked God.

"Just live it."

And then in the middle of the book, I came to a few sentences in the essay, "A Gentle Calling," that tore the very fabric of my being. I don't know which of the essays will strike you in the same way, ripping away hypotheses. But this one settled on the very seam I was sewing:

Why do I write? What am I doing? Where am I going? If I can't get my work published (as seems to be my present condition), should I destroy it, as not good enough? When there is no audience, no reward, shouldn't I burn my failed, unpublishable works? I have experienced so many rejections, so many humiliations! I have also had success (success is better). I am an elder woman now. Yet still, regrets at opportunities not taken, misgivings, doubts, loss of confidence nag me, as they nag every artist, everywhere. Sometimes I reach the limits of my despair and then, as Margaret remarks, "I want to go home, follow God around the house."

That's the background for my shift of perception. Reading, I came to the advice of her grandmother, to *"find an artistic outlet that did not depend on being hired to create."* And *"to find something you love to do, whether it is recognized and supported by the world or not, a passion that will feed your soul in the lean times."*

Oh! Yes! That's why I write. Because of love. It's not about getting published (or not only about that). Again and again she points to a wider reality: "Jesus, the Buddha, Socrates, Epictetus appear never to have picked up the pen, never to have put their names to any writing." If making money is the point, then Steve Jobs trumps Jesus, which is manifestly absurd. Confidently, with a clear head, we can learn to revere what she calls "the willingness to be small." We can learn to be the kind of person who listens, who does not need to see its name on anything, nor expects to be honored, remembered or praised, who wishes to leave behind no mark but the effects of kindness.

I needed that reminder, the jolt of a wider perspective.

So for another day I won't burn the manuscripts that failed. She reminds me that this anguish, this constant self-doubting is the normal state of the creative artist. As an artist, I, too, get to bob between optimism and pessimism (she names her doubting pessimism Bob), despair and joy; and maybe feeling all the emotions is all we're asked to do: live it all.

HER RELATIONSHIP TO animals is especially compelling, and you can't read about her dogs, Flash, Happy, Tater, or her lost cat, Button, or the feral cats she picks up, or the owl, or seeing the spirit of an animal after it has passed over, without a *frisson*—that, yes, at some deep, unremembered level we've seen it, we know it to be true. Can we remember?

I have one final comment, one finger pointing out happily her unique quirkiness. The structure of these essays wander, like life itself, across fields of possibility, arriving at the end with surprising conclusions. I say like life, for I've noticed how I may decide on a straight-path plan and think I'm working toward its execution, while the Universe sets down detours, U-turns, figure-eight roadblocks, rivers and marshes to wade or evade, all of which lead somehow to the goal. Not on my time-frame, and not by the direct route I would have chosen: but always somehow better. So, returning to her essays, consider, for example, Chapter 13, "Necessary Souls," chosen at random. It begins with a story about her first grade teacher, moves to her disdain for authority and Emerson's dictum that you must "trust yourself; every heart vibrates to that iron string." It meanders on to fields of intercessionary prayer, grace, faith, a clairvoyant who told her to wait for her husband-to-be, turns a sharp corner to the consideration of despair, followed by a Presence walking at her side, and finally to a second psychic who, spontaneously bringing up that encounter with the comforting Presence, added that it was St. Theresa of Avila who had come that day.

"And the point? The confirmation of divine attendance, that we are not alone. "Our sorrows, goals, frustrations, fears, even our joys are held. . . by whom? I'm not sure that it matters. By another, by one other, by more than just ourselves."

It's a message I cannot hear too often. Living in the noisy city I need to be reminded again and again (as in these essays) to slow down. Pause. Savor the moment. Attend to the words of Mahatma Ghandi that "There's more to life than speeding up."

To sum up: It is my pleasure to bring you Margaret Dulaney's essays. Reading her, you enter a magical world. It's one you may recognize, but because of her insight, her storytelling, it's shiny-new, optimistic, and mysterious.

—SOPHY BURNHAM

Prologue

I've been writing for half of my life. I would have started earlier but it took me that long to learn to read.

There were several advantages to growing up with a learning disability (which in my case had to do with reading and writing). Competing for rock bottom of my class served to keep me humble, and therefore curious. But, more important, my education left me pretty much unscathed by the tyranny of proper sentence structure (I hear my good editor groan), and unperturbed by the inability to spell (a quality, I understand, I share with Shakespeare).

Every early teacher who had me in her class—and most of them were very kind and patient—wrote the same comment on my twice-yearly reports: "Margaret is a well-meaning girl, but her head is always out the window."

"Oh, but it makes so much more sense out there!" I

would answer in retrospect now, if I could, "Trees don't confuse, birds don't baffle. Give me simple, clear things to learn like the roll of the hills, the turning of the seasons, and I will be as learned as the rest of them. Give me a field, a patch of woodland to read and I will unlock the wisdom of the ages, break the shackles of ignorance! Of course my head is out the window! You have to be in the woods to hear the forest sing!"

My happiest hours during those years were spent in the deep deciduous woods of Kentucky, and my unhappiest hours crept by behind the little wooden flip-top desks in elementary school.

Having difficulties with reading as a child made reading for pleasure vitally important. If reading was going to be as challenging as it was for me, I required a good degree of passion to plow through my learning obstacles. I was eventually to discover that it did not matter how complex the book I was given to read, I would persevere provided I loved the content. An early favorite was The Odyssey. I took to the Greeks and most of Shakespeare like a duck to water, and left the other, anemic material on shore.

When I finally left the world of conventional education in my early twenties, and took full responsibility for my reading life, I dove into the classics of the mid-eighteen hundreds, most notably Charles Dickens and George MacDonald, both of whom seemed to me to write with celestial force. I read each book as slowly as possible, and many of them three and four times over.

In my early thirties I was introduced to the writings

of Ralph Waldo Emerson, and knew from my first encounter that this was a philosophy that I could embrace for a lifetime, a perennial wisdom that challenged me to find my own view of God, but only if I promised to toss that idea aside at the arrival of another, more loving one.

At some point during this period, I remember announcing to my young husband, "I have decided that I will never again read a book that doesn't have God in it."

"I'm not sure you can say that," was Matt's reply.

After suggesting that he might substitute the word *Love* for *God*, I went on to explain that I had grown highly sensitive to the difference between works that were written for love, and those written because the writer fancied himself clever. The latter category I have never been able to suffer for more than a paragraph.

I will choose love over erudition any day. I will read anyone's heartfelt encounter with God: personal epiphanies, near-death experiences, religious ecstasies, angelic visitations. Whatever the quality of the writing, if I sense the love and truth behind the words, I eagerly consume. This eagerness for even the slightest peek at the workings of the heavens, has led me to the works of the great mystics and lovers of all faiths, and eventually had me yearning to add my own cup of truth to this ocean of spiritual writing.

For the first two decades after school, Matt and I lived in New York City, a place that would let us pursue our careers, though it was frustratingly far from the natural world. My fantasies during this period revolved around daylight walks in the country, nights spent with

Matt in front of a quiet fire, with a dog or two, a cat, and a pile of books.

Once, during this exile from the natural world, my mother and I had gone on vacation together and discovered the joy of rising before dawn to take a long walk before breakfast. I had never felt so full of life, so glad.

After eighteen years of city living, in the mid-nineties, my dream was realized. We moved to the rural, rolling hills of Bucks County, Pennsylvania, where we acquired a dog, and then two, a cat, and a neighboring park. When my mother came to visit for our first Thanksgiving, she went off for a walk on her own, and returned to describe a path she had found through the woods. "It's long and well-marked," she said, "with a loop that takes you along the creek at the bottom of the canyon."

"Are you sure that is where you were?" I questioned, "I don't think that there is a path on that side of the park." I was wrong, and can't thank her enough for the discovery. I can be found somewhere along this solitary path every morning, noodling along in a tranquil reverie, praying, listening, noticing, spacing out, and occasionally howling for absent dogs. I am on my fourth dog now, have launched thousands of prayers up through the wood's canopy, seen almost every woodland and creek creature possible and watched the trees grow and tumble. No weather deters me, although my dogs sometimes give me incredulous looks as we head out the door in a blizzard.

I am nearing the end of my second decade of woods

walking, and I would say that little in my life has had such a profound effect on me as this daily practice.

In the beginning I walked and pondered, walked and pondered, walked and pondered. After several years of this exercise I began to walk and ponder and then return home to write. I walked and pondered and wrote, walked and pondered and wrote for many more years until I had amassed a collection of spiritual writings. For the next several years I walked and pondered and wrote and prayed for a way to share my musings with an audience. I must admit, this chapter of my life seemed a tad interminable.

One day, having exhausted an army of ideas of where to find publication for my writings, I sat in my backyard, pencil in hand, frustrated, staring at the old bank barn at the edge of our property, when a thought appeared in my mind. "Hm, there's a recording studio in my backyard,"—my husband had converted our ancient stone barn into a studio a decade earlier for his record label—"I wonder if the pleasure of being read to is as precious to others as it is to me?"

The experience of being read to as a child inspired a life-long practice of reading and listening to books read aloud. My siblings and I read to one another through our teens and into our twenties, and my husband and I have carried on the tradition throughout our life together. I consider being read to a fine luxury, and the idea of offering this pleasure to those outside my immediate family felt perfectly right.

This was the birth of Listen Well, a website that offers one ten-minute, recorded piece of writing a month to a community of listening souls.

Over the seven years since the site's conception I have occasionally received written communications from my listeners. This is always a lovely reminder of why I write, why I ponder, why I walk. The circle completes itself, and every step along my path feels blessed.

Several of my listeners have asked whether I planned to publish a written collection of some of my writings. This book is an answer to this inquiry, with a bonus of a few unrecorded writings.

I offer it in gratitude for every listening ear.

Holding Hands
and Climbing

I

The Good Student

The writer Joan Grant believed that every human being was both teacher and pupil, and that at any moment we are both instructing someone and learning from someone else, with one always behind and one ahead. Humanity, she said, was moving forward en masse into enlightenment. But, she warned, the instant any single member of this interdependent progression stopped learning, he would in turn lose his ability to teach. This refusal to learn would gum up the works, so to speak, and the united movement toward awakening would hesitate, would falter.

I would add that those near the same level of learning will alternate between acting as teacher and pupil for one another, shifting positions, tossing the learning ball back and forth. In this generous exchange of lesson and learning, the open, curious personality is most valuable, and the pedantic know-it-all becomes a hindrance. An arrogant temperament causes evolutionary gridlock. It does no good to honk your horn, yell out the window, because the person who has stopped learning can move neither forward nor backward. Their frozen attitude has created a maddening pile-up of stalled souls.

So it would appear that the short list of qualities most valuable for the student to cultivate would be as follows: curiosity (always the top of the list), a willingness to learn (paramount), the ability to listen, to remain still and quiet, to cooperate with the rest of the students, to be able to listen (did I mention this?). I won't go into what it is that makes for a difficult student. I assume most of us have lived these attributes, and suffered the consequences. Each has been sent to the principal's office, been held back, chewed out, flunked out, skipped out, failed, failed, and failed again.

OVER THE COURSE of my adult life, I have had a series of dreams about school. The metaphor is always crystal clear. There have been more dreams than I care to mention where I was unable to graduate from high school and several where I searched for a school where I might feel more comfortable than the one in which I was enrolled, one where I might feel I belonged. I believe I share with the rest of the human race dreams where I have never gone to French class and am expected to take the final exam (I presume the French dream the same of English class). Of course this is always at times when I'm feeling overwhelmed and ill prepared for the duties of the next day. The recent years have been a relatively joyous time of my life and not long ago I had a dream where I was standing at the base of a gently sloping, verdant mountain. Next to me stood my grandmother, who graduated from this world and into the eternal one in 1988. "I'm going to the most beautiful school!" I told her. "It's on the top of that gorgeous mountain, and I am so happy there!" Happy, yes, but still in school, always in school.

The idea of being a student helps me to be less disapproving of myself and, I hope, of others. When someone makes a choice that I feel is unwise, it's useful to think, "maybe the course load was too much for him." Being judgmental of a friend's journey is like faulting a seven-year-old for attending primary school. "Oh that so-in-so, she is just soooo second grade."

Many of us seem able to take college level courses in some areas of our lives but struggle through middle school in others—those who are a whiz in math but sorely in need of remedial reading, for example, or those who are responsible at work but irresponsible in love. The well-rounded, master-of-all-disciplines is nonexistent, I would venture, and it's simply illogical to be overly critical of another's weak subjects. "Poor thing has fallen behind in social studies," we might observe. "He'll catch up eventually," we could add, "even if it takes three hundred years."

Some of us overestimate our abilities. "She never should have taken on so many credits," we could say of a friend who isn't able to complete an assignment, which could be anything from not showing up for a lunch date to raising her ten children.

I suspect most of us are under the illusion that one day we will complete our schooling, graduate and really be something, be someone whole, a perfectly responsible, respectable, adult.

I have never met such a phenomenon, myself.

Under the circumstances, the path to higher education seems to require us to be very patient with our own and others' failings.

"Out of a great need we are all holding hands and climbing," the Sufi poet Hafiz writes. *"Not loving is a letting go. Listen, the terrain around here is far too dangerous for that."*

ALTHOUGH I CANNOT claim a fundamental membership in any religion, I have a deep respect for what I believe to be fundamental to all of them. I've given years of effort, for instance, to bouncing around the contents of the Lord's Prayer. The appeal that inspires the liveliest brain calisthenics is: "Forgive us our trespasses as we forgive those who trespass against us." I love the choice of the word "trespass," and can't bear the newer translation that substitutes the word "debt." How dare they! I could be one of those zealots, a tear-away who starts her own sect over the removal of the word trespass from the

Lord's Prayer. But really, the word "debt" is so vague, so open to interpretation. Now "trespass," that is a word. We know when we're trespassing, when we've marched past all of the signs and are having a messy picnic all over someone else's soul. After some loud belching and grass smashing, we slink off, leaving our trash behind.

It therefore makes sense that we only ask for the degree of forgiveness that we are willing to muster for another, after our own souls have been rutted up by the deep tire tracks of trespass. "Forgive us as we forgive." Hence, if we are very stingy with our own forgiveness it seems fair that we accept only so much as we're willing to hand out.

Here's a question: is it possible to trespass against our own selves? Does an alcoholic trespass on the temple of his body, leaving sticky beer cans and stupid words all over the floor? Do we trespass on our souls when we are unfairly self-critical? Do we not roll our own front yards with toilet paper with this sort of mental activity?

Furthermore, is it possible to trespass by NOT taking action? When we don't call a friend to offer help, knowing it is the right thing to do, have we not neglected to water all of the lovely flowers we gathered on her property? I know I have begged forgiveness for non-action, when I knew action to be the right thing.

And lastly, does a superpower trespass by ignoring the horrors of ethnic cleansing in another country? Is it possible to trespass on the gracious grounds of humanitarianism?

A lifetime of careful consideration of this one supplication from the Lord's Prayer could bring us very near the gardens of enlightenment. Somehow I am convinced that enlightenment IS occurring on this planet, no matter how much the news tries to persuade me otherwise. Yes, there are still horrible trespasses (child beating, torture, more slavery than ever), but the difference is, most moderate people in most countries know these practices to be great wrongs, and those who indulge in them do so covertly. For too many years we justified such conduct: "Spare the rod, spoil the child." "Of course we have slaves, how else would we have cotton?" and more recently, "But we have to make him talk, how else will we know the enemy?"

Some people believe that there is a certain amount of light and dark in the world and nothing we can do will ever alter the ratio. I have many issues with this philosophy, the principal being that if I were to adopt such a view, it would render me bedridden. It would be as if I were being asked to spend the rest of my life in third grade, endlessly repeating the same lessons. I would rebel; hold my breath until I turned blue and passed out (of the world, that is). I have to live with a measure of hope for the progress of mankind, or else risk hardening into a lump of petrified indifference.

I wonder how many, like myself, are bone-weary of cynicism. You hear its dark rumblings daily: "You can't trust a politician." "Nothing ever changes." "Corporations are all out to get you." "There will always be war, starvation, foolish class systems." Perhaps, but like slavery, torture and the beating of children, we begin first by suspecting these to be wrongs, and watch as they become embarrassments. This seems to be the natural consequence of dirty practice. Someday I imagine all conflict with arms will be seen as shameful behavior, and our good soldiers will truly wage peace instead of war.

Some consider those who believe in the possibility of world peace to be naïve; those who trust that the earth can feed all of its inhabitants, idealistic; those who visualize the planet's return to health, simplistic. "Not in our lifetime," you hear. But of course, enlightenment is an unfolding, not a destination. There are centuries yet to travel.

The puzzle is how so many of us in the developed world who consider ourselves at least somewhat enlightened can still, quite innocently, trespass, and do so almost hourly. I say this as a marginal citizen of the United States (some days praising, some days criticizing) who wishes to be a stellar citizen of Planet Earth. There is simply so much for us to learn, so many ways in which we stomp all over the planet, leaving our beer cans and cigarette butts. There are hundreds of choices, which we make daily, that have huge, far-reaching consequences: our obsessive upgrading of gadgets, creating mountains of toxic trash, our wasteful consumption of 30 percent of the world's resources, our shameless complaints, as so much of the world struggles under the profound weight of extreme poverty.

When do my unthinking choices become trespasses? The list, I fear, is daunting, but this is no reason to claim ignorance and throw up my hands. It is more reason to continue to search for ways to improve. I'd like to believe that I have at least enough enlightenment to begin to root out the ignorant in my daily choices. Someday, I hope to feel myself less a trespasser and more an invited guest on this gracious planet.

It does help me to believe that I was meant to partake of life on the planet in my shifting roles as student and teacher, not hoping to achieve anything more glorious than a more enlightened soul. It lessens the pressures of the day.

Yet I must admit to having worthless days, days when I simply cannot fathom what I am doing with my existence, as if everyone around me were busy pushing along the evolution of life but me.

If you have ever shared even a hint of this dreary speculation, we both are in good company. Ralph Waldo Emerson, for example, felt the weight of such days. "Yonder uplands are rich pasturage, and my neighbor has fertile meadow, but my field, says the querulous farmer, only holds the world together."

What I find fascinating about the workings of the world is how often, when I'm in such a glum mood, some opportunity of usefulness will be unexpectedly handed to me.

Many years ago, before I had animals of my own (or I should say, before I began to pack my home full of animals), I was having a dreadful attack of uselessness. My husband and I had newly moved to the country and I had no friends, as well as no animals, to take care of. I had been wandering around in my back yard in a fog of paralyzing self-negation, circling through a list of empty pursuits, of vacuous reasons for my existence. Finally, weary of my damp, dead-end thinking, I asked to be given some sign of worth, some small signal of my life's necessity.

Moments later a dog bounded into my back yard from out of the woods.

The yard at the time had a good deal going on in it. My husband had been overseeing the building of a fence along the road by our house and there were several men standing around in various states of work and discussion.

When the dog entered the yard, he raced past this group of men, practically leaping over them, in an apparent frenzy to reach me where I stood near the back screen door. He was long-legged and fast and in such a mad fury to get to me, and taking so little notice of the others that it occurred to me that he might have mistaken me for a large squirrel. Surely, I reasoned in that brief instant, he was about to execute his instinctual designs by shaking me by my scrawny neck. In a sudden panic, I ankled it through the back screen door, just before the dog, unable to stop his enthusiastic trajectory, threw himself against it. He recovered, partially, and stood panting and staring at the door. I hotfooted it around to another room, and looked out a window that would allow me to study him without his notice, and perhaps detect, from a point of relative safety, any signs of rabies or mad cow disease. Somehow he sensed my presence, turned to my window and raced over, placing his great paws on the windowsill to peer in.

I asked him, through the safety of the window, why he didn't just go out and find one of the men who were working in the yard. I suggested that he might find the men less defensive of their necks, and therefore more inclined to listen. Without a glance in the men's direction, he stared fixedly into my eyes, allowing me to make a more studied assessment. He was a mixed breed, of the largish, shepherd-like variety—faintly curling tail, long wolfish nose. He wore a rather dear, albeit anxious expression. He did not look the least like a hardened assassin. His name, if I had been asked to give him one on the spot, might have been Buddy, or Clem, something friendly, harmless... ok, even loveable.

I sighed, walked around to the door, opened it and stepped out to see what I could do for him. This caused such fireworks of desperate joy that it took quite a while to read the wildly dangling ID tag, which landed and shot out of my hand a hundred times. Finally able to detect a phone number, I hunted for a pen, hunted for a piece of paper, hunted for the phone, while the dog continued to circle and leap, allowing less than two inches to come between us. The phone call prompted an equally mad fit of joy from his owner, a mother, who told me how many torturous days he had been missing and how much his child housemates had wept since his absence. She came at once, eliciting wails of gladness from both parties, and the circle of losing and finding was complete. I rung with gratitude for hours afterward.

This whole scenario took perhaps twenty minutes and was entirely lost on the men at the fence project.

Months later when I mentioned the lost dog story to my husband, he was completely clueless. "Dog?" he asked, "in our yard?" The incident had clearly been intended for me.

I don't mean to imply that the loss of the dog and the subsequent anxiety of his family occurred just for my benefit. I tell this story because I believe it illustrates the remarkably intricate design that weaves all of our needs into such a fine pattern that if one were able to follow each thread backwards through the complexity of connection and miracle, the exercise would blow our tiny little finite minds.

In other words, if you took the thread of my own dreary thinking, the thread of the dog's fearful journey, the thread of misery around the loss of the dog from each member of the dog's household, if you took these threads and attempted to follow them back even a few days, you could never unravel the wisdom behind this happening.

This fabric of cause and effect seems to be fabulously complex and dense, dense like the deep pile of a thick rug. And, although there have been moments in my life where I believed I had discovered a worn spot, where I detected a bit of light shining through, I suspect the relative shining is like that of a candle next to the sun.

I will take that candle for now, take it gratefully.

2

My Name Is Margaret
and I'm About to be Five

The discovery that I had managed to successfully incarnate came upon me quite suddenly and with such clarity that, even though it has been well over forty years, the memory remains one of my sharpest mental snapshots to date.

I stood alone in the den of my family's house and, with my hand resting on my mother's desk, announced to my companionless surroundings: "My name is Margaret and I am about to be five." I have other certain memories in my life but none return in such sharp outline as this one. The proclamation seemed to embrace so much at once: my soul's complete arrival, my given identity for this go around, and—perhaps not so obvious—my commitment to stick around for a while.

From this moment on I began to collect memory. Indeed, everything before this moment is hidden from me, as if from an un-retrieved dream.

The very size of this occurrence, in the retelling, in contrast to its effect, has caused me much deliberation over the years. These *"announcements of the soul"* as Emerson has coined them, have always arrived for me in the smallest of packages. Perhaps this is because the Heavens have it figured out that, had it been otherwise, I would have been an insufferable, proselytizing bore, knocking on doors and handing out printed pamphlets.

I remember reading with keen disappointment the story of C. S. Lewis's spiritual conversion, *Surprised By Joy*. I kept waiting for the fireworks, but none came. In fact, I have noted that none of my spiritual teachers in print, C.S. Lewis, Ralph Waldo Emerson, George Mac-Donald, Marcus Aurelius, to name just a few, have ever wowed me with their awakenings. This doesn't, however, keep me from longing for pyrotechnics in my own life. It hasn't stopped me from craving those mighty apparitions with choral underscoring, visiting angels with recognizable names, huge heavenly hands reaching down for divine rearrangement, but the more I desire these cosmic theatrics, the tinier my "announcements" become.

At the end of childhood and the beginning of adulthood I had an announcement of a very different sort. Whereas the initial one seemed an awakening to separation, this I believe, was an awakening to connection.

One evening, while visiting a friend in the country, I

stood out on a hillside, alone, watching the stars. It had been a particularly difficult period in my life where despair seemed to hound my every quiet moment, a condition that I had been attempting to alleviate with constant company. Therefore the fact that I was completely alone at this time could be considered mystery enough. However I came to be in this solitary state, there I stood, on the little hill behind the house, looking up at the night sky. Now this, I must warn, is where the story grows vague. Gently, ever so gently, I was aware of a presence, a real, very individual presence. I was given no name and I did not jump, nor have I ever wished to jump, to any conclusive idea of who this presence might have been. A friend's mother, in the last months of her life, reported to having met the Buddha in her bathroom. Although I can find no grounds to disbelieve her, I can make no such claims of my own. In my readings since this time, the closest term I have found to name this presence is the Sufi expression, the Beloved. This presence, merely by its proximity on my little hill, seemed to create of me another Beloved, seemed to wish to share this quality with me, so that we seemed to be one Beloved together. I have no idea how long I remained in the company of this presence, but when I returned to the house and my friends, I was altered, and lay awake all night with the exhilaration of this meeting.

I begin to see now that I have lived my life, slowly, ever so faintly, gaining awareness of, and too often losing sight of, this presence. But I believe that every year, by just the slightest margin, my awareness has grown. As if that evening, on the hillside, a path opened to me where previously I had seen only forest, a path that I have been stumbling along for the past thirty years.

In George MacDonald's novel, *The Marquis of Lossie*, The teacher is asked by his student, *"How is it that you know there is a God, and one fit to be trusted as you trust him?"* He replies, *"Namely, that all my difficulties and confusions have gone on clearing themselves up ever since I set out to walk in that way. My consciousness of life is threefold what it was; my perception of what is lovely around me, and my delight in it, threefold; my power of understanding things and of ordering my way, threefold also; the same with my hope and my courage, my love to my kind, my power of forgiveness. In short, I cannot but believe that my whole being and its whole world are in process of rectification for me."* No pyrotechnics there.

At the end of each year, I try and sift back through the moments where this presence has revealed itself to me. I have given up looking for the thunderous and search only for the those quiet, tiptoeing revelations that I have learned to recognize. One year the means of this revelation was so small it could fit into the cupped palms of one's hands.

I was living in New York at the time with my then adolescent dog. One morning, while walking this dog in Washington Square Park, I noticed a pigeon behaving oddly near the tops of the trees. She would attempt to fly out from one of the trees, just above the central sidewalk, jerk suddenly to a stop, and then travel, as if dragged, in a low arc back to the tree. On closer inspection I could see that the pigeon's feet were tangled in the end of a long length of plastic fishing line. In following the line from the bird, I could see that, after thirty feet or so, it was wrapped around a high branch of a tree and, after another thirty, its end was knotted around the wooden slats of one of the park benches. I couldn't imagine how this had come to be, but the sight of the bird repeating this futile attempt to free herself was terribly sorrowful to witness.

It was very early and there were few people in the park, and of those few, none seemed to be paying the least attention to this dismal scene. I tied my dog to a nearby bench, whose growing interest in the low swinging bird made this a difficult task, and moved to the spot where the fishing line was attached. I pulled at the line, which was very thick and well secured, with absolutely no effect, as my dog's curiosity began to consume her. I pulled harder and called out to passersby to inquire whether anyone might have something on them with which to cut the line, a knife, for example, but no one came forward with such an item—a fact which should quiet the fears of anyone planning on visiting New York. A couple of times the bird, in her low, sorrowful arc back to the tree nearly skimmed the snapping jaws of my now half-crazed canine. I tugged and tugged at the line, which dug into my flesh, as my dog proceeded to lose her mind and I my faith in human compassion.

The fact did occur to me that I had no plan for removing the line from the feet of the bird, once I managed to snap the line, and there was a very real chance that, once released, she might fall into the gaping mouth of my now psychotic retriever. However delightful this conclusion might have been for my dog, it would have been a rather disquieting one to me, but I had to admit, this seemed a kinder fate than the repetition of hope and despair that the bird was suffering at the present.

At some point I gave up entirely on humanity lending me a hand and put all of my effort into breaking the line. After several furious jerks, and just as the bird had completed her outward journey and was at the end of her tether, about forty feet above the sidewalk, I was able to snap the line. At the same time the bird gave up her struggle and began to fall, only this time, instead of swooping, wings spread, back toward the tree, she glided straight down. I turned to watch her landing, imagining a multitude of horrible scenarios, when suddenly, as if by magic, a man appeared beneath her. I assume that in my frantic tuggings I hadn't seen him approach. He was middle-aged, handsome, and sharply dressed in a well-tailored suit. A man, I remember thinking, whom I could very well imagine representing me in a court of law, but not a man who would willingly handle a city pigeon. I stood frozen, as if ordered to do so, and watched.

As though their actions had been previously choreographed, the man stopped, looked above his head, held out his clean, cupped hands and waited, while my bird, with perfect precision, landed inside of them. Without the slightest hesitation on the man's part and without any sign of fear on the bird's, he very gently untied the line from her tiny, still legs, and lifted her into the air and into freedom. After pausing for just a moment to assure himself of her sound flight, he walked away, leaving me and my bewildered Labrador panting in disbelief.

From the instant this man came into my sight until he left it, he never once glanced in my or my lunatic dog's direction, never appeared to acknowledge that we were any part of the bird's story. He stepped in and out of the final act of our little drama as a god would in a Greek tragedy, stepped in and out and didn't stick around for the curtain call. Watching him walk away, I wouldn't have been the least surprised to see him sprout wings of his own and take flight.

There have been a number of instances where I believe I have been given a glimpse into the intricate workings of the heavens, where the Beloved has tipped his hand, so to speak, and I have been allowed to see the machinations of the perfect design. I imagine these glimpses are judged to be just the right size for me, for though these occurrences have not been earth-shaking and huge, worthy of a printed pamphlet, they have seemed to me as full of the truth of an ever-present divinity as the night sky is of stars.

Looking back over my life from little story to little story, looking back as if looking at the night sky, each story appears as a tiny spark of the divine visible. As the first story suggested my own place, my own necessity in this sky full of stars, all the rest, the hundred little sparkly stories that have followed seem to point to the miracle of the design, and my dependence on the ordering of this perfection. And while I long for meteor showers and supernovas, above me hang these exquisite heavenly objects. Visible without straining is this firmament of little glimpses into the divine.

3

Good Listening

When I was in fourth grade, my teacher, address-ing our class, exclaimed with astonishment, "You have all progressed so nicely this year, you should be proud of yourselves. Even Margaret is able to read out loud."

For much of my life I was so dreamy that such com-ments skipped lightly off my psyche. This one only vaguely got my attention. "Gosh," I thought, "I really must be slow." I was tested and studied for many years: my eyes, my hand to eye coordination, my IQ. No one could quite figure me out. They would label me with a learning disability now, no doubt, but at that time, I was just considered a bit behind the rest. I plodded along in the slow reading group, distracted, occasionally completely lost, and sometimes understanding.

My sister Janey, four years older than I, used to help me with my homework and ended up working in early education, primarily, she tells me, because she had witnessed my struggle with mainstream teaching practices and suspected that there would have been better ways of handling me. She believes that she could have taught me how to write legibly. My handwriting was, and still is, that of a half-human three-year-old. I wonder if she could have taught me how to spell—I am so challenged by spelling that I often rip up grocery lists in despair.

It wasn't until I left school, and no one was telling me what to read, no one was rushing me, that I picked up a book with quiet, unhurried focus. That book was *David Copperfield*. Once I became responsible for my choice of reading material, I began to seriously absorb the written word.

My pace in reading has never picked up, in fact, just the opposite. It has slowed to a glacial tempo, not only because I simply cannot read swiftly, but because I am loath to move forward until I have thoroughly savored every nuance. I know now the amount of editing and sweat that can be visited on one paragraph, one sentence, one word. It would seem terribly ungrateful of me to hurry, to skim. "But, what if the material is not worth the second read?" one might ask, "beach reading, for instance?" I cannot bear such writing. If you find it shallow at a swift swim, imagine it at a plodding doggy paddle! Insufferable!

In my early twenties I discovered paragraphs among Charles Dickens' enormous offering that I knew better than to wade through only once. For some twice was not sufficient, for others not even three times. Or, let me put it this way: I could have read them once, but I suspected that when I eventually arrived at the pearly gates, Saint Peter would be sure to greet me with grave disappointment, and so would Lao Tzu, and perhaps Emerson, yes, Ralph Waldo would be there. I don't think Dickens would bother to show up. No, why would he? But these other guys, they'd be there and they'd all be shaking their heads, exasperated.

"Oh, dear," Saint Peter would sigh, "I'm afraid you'll have to go back down there."

I don't think any good thing should be hurried: a good meal, conversation, book, view, laugh, cry, day, chapter, life.

Challenging as my early schooling had been, I was ultimately grateful for having been a slow child, a slow student, a slow reader. Not only do I believe that this pace has aided in teaching me how to write—imagine a painter dashing through the Louvre, madly counting the number of paintings he can see in two hours—but this measured tempo was probably preparing me for my greatest learning, for attempting to perfect the most precious of talents: that of listening. Listening is such a generous gift. It feeds everyone. At some point we all long to be heard, even if just by one quiet ear. Being heard is essential to the process of self-discovery. It shapes destinies, spreads enlightenment, betters the world. I would love at the end of my life to have acquired its genius.

Listening, however, is a highly refined art, difficult to master.

People say things like this: "I will make them listen." Impossible. You can make them stop talking, but you cannot make them listen.

Or this: "I will force myself to listen." Another impossibility.

And, I'm sure we've all thought this: "I need to focus on what he is saying." Focus implies force, and force requires effort. Listening, true listening cannot be forced. Listening is an allowing. It is like falling to sleep. It is a letting go.

I have noticed that this surrender, this letting go is particularly necessary when listening to someone in another language, or even to a very heavy accent. If I am straining to understand, understanding will not come. If I relax and wait for the understanding, it arrives, as if by magic.

You cannot pour tea into a moving cup.

If you wish to learn the art of listening, try and hold the mind still. Hold it gently, and wait. There's time enough. There's always enough time, an eternity of time.

I'VE BEEN THINKING a lot lately about eternity. Funny how a single day feels when you're convinced you have an infinite number of them. I've always believed in life

eternal (an early gift from my family), but have only recently acquired a relatively eternal view of my present
existence. And, since I'm not convinced this view is going to remain as clear as it is now, given the changeable
weather of my mind, I thought I would write myself a
little note as a reminder. Tuck away a little memento
while the sky is this cloudless, the sun this high.

I've had a recurring dream since I left high school in
which I'm being informed that I, in fact, never graduated
and have to repeat my senior year. I've had this dream so
often I can't begin to count. At some point during the
dream I become aware of my present age. "You mean,
I've lived in five different homes, been married for over
twenty years, suffered flesh-melting hot flashes," I marvel, "and I still haven't managed to complete my senior
year in high school?!" I spend the rest of the dream
searching for a boarding school (yes, for some reason it
must be a boarding school) that will have me along with
my middle-aged husband, my abundance of house pets,
my horse and my well-seasoned disrespect for authority.
As an amateur analyst, I have always assumed that the
dream had to do with a nagging feeling that I had never
succeeded in accomplishing anything.

Imagine my surprise last week when I woke up in the
middle of the night having dreamt that I had just graduated. I lay in the wee-hour quiet in perfect contentment,
my dream-diploma resting lightly in my dream-hand.

The morning after my dream-commencement, with
a clear, caffeine-swept head, I understood its significance. It wasn't that I'd finally attained some newswor-

thy accomplishment, that I was now able to pronounce my profession, religion, identifying summation, that I could now give bold answer to that pesky cocktail party question, "What do you do?" It wasn't that I could reply without hesitation: Oh, I am a writer, transcendentalist, Christian-Buddhist, empathic-compassionist (I made up that last bit, but like it). The reason that I'd finally been given my dream-diploma, I believe, was that I had somehow grasped the idea that inherent in the gift of each day was an eternity of uses for my quirky, inimitable individuality. After all, how could one begin to harness the potential of a single soul on its eternal voyage in a single day?

I have many friends who chafe against the idea that there is a reason for everything that happens to us. I can sympathize with this resistance. How often have I related some painful story of supreme suffering, and instead of meeting with compassion been leveled by the pseudo-cheerful phrase, "Well, there must be a reason!"

When I say that I am the proud owner of a new eternal view, I don't wish to imply that my vision reaches to infinity and that I now begin to know the reasons behind the world's suffering. But somehow (some might call this grace) I've managed an attitude that allows me to believe that a billion light years from now, I might look back on today's difficulty with the understanding of its necessity. The problem with the dreaded phrase "there must be a reason" is that it hints at a reward/punishment theory that too often looks to the past to condone the misery of the present. I don't wish to undermine the great power of consequences and the use of learning from past mistakes. How else would we grow? The problem is, any justification for suffering delivered from the half-blind vantage point of our finite lives will be maddeningly simplistic.

Several years ago my neighbor's husband died in what seemed an instant. He had gone out in the afternoon to his hunting stand and hadn't returned when it grew dark. His wife asked a neighbor to look for him and he was discovered on the ground, lifeless, having suffered a massive heart attack. My husband and I and four other neighbors raced over to her house and sat with her through that excruciating evening.

If you are ever in the position I and my friends were in that night, I recommend one thing, and this only. As my friend used to suggest to her preschool daughter when she risked spinning out of her mother's control, "Do good listening!"

No amount of philosophy will be of any use. "There must be a reason" or worse, "I guess God just wanted another angel." This sort of saccharine reasoning is not only a low blow to the mourner, but also an insult to God. "Doesn't God have the whole damned universe?" one might question. "Does he really need to take my husband?!" Again, do good listening.

I often think of Michelangelo's prisoners, those half-chiseled beings struggling to emerge from their marble cells that line the antechamber of the Academia in Florence. If you have never had the privilege of visiting this museum I invite you to take a descriptive tour. You enter the building from the bustling Florentine square and walk into a large, silent room filled with massive hunks of rough marble, mined from deep inside some distant mountain. Climbing out of these great stones are half-formed humans, which, through the divine talent of the artist, hint at the as yet unrealized majesty of their fully formed bodies. These semi-humans twist and struggle against their marble prisons, creating an atmosphere of raw tension. Just beyond this turmoil, in the next chamber, standing perfectly, peacefully, gloriously alone is Michelangelo's David—anatomically impossible, god-like, perfectly realized—a holy, holy being. No copy will ever do this work justice. To stand in the presence of this sublime work of art is to grasp its divinity, as if one were able to buy a ticket to look upon a star.

Just before my mother died, I spoke to my stepfather and, for the first time since my mother was diagnosed with Alzheimer's disease nine years earlier, he allowed himself to voice the thought that it was just "so unfair." That she had never been anything but good to others, and therefore why was she chosen out of the great wash of souls for this punishment, to be trapped in the prison of her body? I wanted to answer, "It seems unfair now but we're still in the antechamber, still among the half-chiseled. You won't believe what's in the next room!" But I didn't, of course, instead I did good listening.

Some, out of frustration, conclude that indeed the whole confusing jumble is the result of random chaos, the search for reason and meaning a big waste of time. Although I can understand the temptation of this conclusion, I cannot accept it. I don't believe that the sculptor's chisel is meant to inflict either reward or punishment, or that its blows are delivered without aim, but that each swing of the mallet carries the potential to disclose the ineffable beauty of our spirits. I believe one day, one distant, eternal day, we will all be as beautiful as Michelangelo's David, every single one of us. There have been moments in my life, whole days even, when I have felt the expert hands of the artist.

4

Mary's Story

A neighbor recently said to me, "You sure do take friendship seriously." I wonder whether this was a way of saying I was a busybody. The fact is, once a friend has moved into my orbit, that person is immediately placed on the Endangered Species List, and can expect to be fiercely protected and monitored on a regular basis. This is best accomplished with phone calls, feedings and frequent gatherings.

The poor darlings can't get away from me.

A friend is a luxury, I believe, and mustn't be relied upon as one would a spouse or family member. There will be friends in our lives who will feed us, and some whom we will feed. There will be friends who counsel and those who require counsel. There will be friends who draw us out, and ones who need drawing. Finally there will be friends who will willingly sit with us while we die, and those who simply cannot.

When my mother was in the late stages of Alzheimer's disease there were those who visited and those who couldn't. Many of the latter came up to me at Mother's funeral and made a point of confessing their inability to visit near the end.

"I just couldn't see her like that," they would sheepishly admit.

"There were some who could and some who couldn't," I would respond. "I am not sure, if she were one of my peers, and not my mother, which camp I would fall into," I assured them.

Somehow, I suspect that both responses have their value. It could be that our image of her has a better chance of returning to health and vitality than had it been otherwise. Had all of her friends been intimately involved in those challenging end years, they might be frozen in a state of paralyzing sadness, unable to move on, unwilling to see her as having moved on, unable to view her as eternal.

It's tempting to fall into an unhealthy fixation with the last days of a person's life and lose sight of the vibrant spark, the spirit that for a time enlivened this world. At the same time, I can't imagine that it would be helpful for the soul that is in the process of translating into a new life for those left behind to dwell on the last moments of their dying body. It would seem to weigh down the expanding spirit with the damp, cold stones of sorrow. Mourn the life that was never allowed a chance to lend its light to the world, but not the fleeting moments, in an eternity of moments, when the ailing body struggles to release its irrepressible spirit.

My mother had an attitude toward friendship similar to my own. Like a sheepdog, she would watch over her little lambs, gather them to safety, chase the wolves away.

I adopted this herding tendency and have to watch that I don't lose sight of the shepherd. The shepherd (or whatever it is one wishes to call this guiding spirit) is there to correct, oversee, train his little helpers, and doesn't wish for them to supersede his good counsel with their own notions of what might be best for the flock. "Stay in your role, dear," the shepherd seems to say to me, with a good deal of encouragement and head patting.

The shepherd knows me all too well. There are times when I do not trust this presiding wisdom and plunge into panic. This is when I can be seen racing around in circles, worrying the flock. I spent every weekend of my late twenties and some in my early thirties tending my friends. It became a sort of career for me. My husband and I bought a tiny one-bedroom house in the country, an hour and a half drive from New York City, where we would invite our city-weary, country-hungry friends (or so I saw them). We housed so many friends in those years that we were forced to bed some of them down in closets. I would gather them, fuss over them, feed them. It was a joyful pursuit, but ultimately unsustainable. I needed to find my own job, and not try to do the job of the shepherd. The flock would survive without me.

Although I have relaxed this weekly effort, I would still call myself a foul weather friend, dashing in with extra raingear to save those I know from any discomfort. I cannot bear the sight of one of my friends wandering off alone. I corral the poor things together in haphazard flocks hoping they will meet their next best friend, their true love. I once introduced a pair who fell in love, moved in with each other within weeks—much to my satisfaction—and parted just minutes before they murdered one another. Both went on to meet their better matches.

I begin to suspect that this meddling of mine is not always so welcome to the heavens and their divine plans. I can only imagine the celestial irritation when a carefully organized lesson plan has to be tossed out because of my interference. When I race into a friend's life to hold off all suffering, all loneliness, is this not enormously frustrating to the designer of these perfectly orchestrated teachings? In some cases these lessons appear to have been in the design process since birth!

"Damn, here she comes again!" I hear the angels lament, "screwing up all of our hard work!"

Of course there are times when a friend must intercede in another's life, when there is a clear signal from the shepherd, when we are called to do so. But, the tricky part is being able to read the signs. I have noticed that the older dogs are better at this than the younger ones. "Hold back," they seem to say when a member of the flock falls, "give them time, the chance to lift themselves, or they will never find their legs."

These elder ones have learned to wait, eyes trained on the shepherd, alert, eager, expectant, as willing to leap into action as they are to be held back. There are circumstances that call for action, and others that suggest passive prayer and observation.

I'm feeling more and more like an old dog these days.

I HAVE A friend that I will call Mary.

Every morning Mary wakes, leaps out of bed and powers through a mad-activity-packed day until, completely spent, she dives back under the covers. She's self-employed, self-motivated, enthusiastic, curious, driven, chatty, gregarious, funny, vivacious, ambitious, and happy.

Over the years of unchecked driving energy, Mary has developed a condition that has the medical community baffled. What began as small outbreaks of skin rash has, over the span of about twenty years, developed into mystifying episodes of swelling body parts: one ear, a shoulder, her lower lip, and more recently joints and muscles, resulting in random days and sleepless nights of intense pain, a malady that Mary comically refers to as her swell-up disease, but that I know is seriously taking its toll on her quality of life.

Mary's unremitting engine, however, continues to roar, as her poor, fragile body rattles and sputters, threatening to break down entirely. My suspicion is that her battered nervous system just can't handle all of that effervescence.

Having attempted to trail Mary though a typical day, I have learned to quit by lunch and nap until dinner.

A consumer of culture, Mary rarely turns down an opportunity to travel to, learn of, taste the food of, listen to the sounds of another country. During a respite from the more severe symptoms of her disease, Mary and I found ourselves, along with a handful of other friends, traveling to Peru.

OUR TRIP BEGAN and ended in the city of Cusco (gorgeous, gorgeous Cusco) where we stayed in an old monastery that had been converted to a hotel in the 1960's. The Monesterio is an exquisite, rambling, austere, ancient place that seems so full of the hauntings of its previous inhabitants that one can almost hear them as they pad down the corridors to vespers. It houses a perfectly preserved chapel, with religious paintings hanging from every wall (saints and angels, some a tad severe), a sobering contrast to the exuberance of life just outside the hotel doors.

Cusco is full to bursting with vibrant, unrestrained life: women with so much color in their dress they look like birthday presents with their volcano skirts and bright top hats. Everywhere there are llamas, babies, dogs (all happy, well loved and well fed), bright silver, gold, riotous, contrasting color, luscious fabrics, alpaca, wool, small, glad people with gorgeous nut-brown, nut-round, clear faces. The joy of this place is palpable.

The only thing the newly arrived tourist cannot expect to find in Cusco is air. At nearly twelve thousand feet, oxygen is a precious luxury.

"Upon arrival in Cusco," the guidebooks suggest, "it is advisable to go directly to your hotel and lie down."

This is my second time in Cusco. I believe them.

"Many hotels offer cans of oxygen for purchase."

Ours does, that's a comfort.

"It's best to eat lightly, and keep alcohol consumption to a minimum."

Easy to do, my insides feel like they've been crammed into a briefcase.

"Drink plenty of water."

No problem. Is there oxygen in water?

I follow all of the rules, puff up to my hotel room, lie down, stare at the can of oxygen next to my bed and doze off, wake up, hydrate, doze again. When I do move, as far as the bathroom for instance, it is with creeping, turtle-slow movements. There seems no choice in the matter, as three swift steps will cause a knee-grabbing, head-spinning, mad-gasping episode. I feel all the symptoms in the book, but stop short of barfing. I don't believe in barfing.

While I dutifully lie in my horizontal, torpid state, Mary is off dashing around town, touching every fabric, chatting up the store owners, snapping photos, eating food from street vendors, petting dogs, soaking up every sight and sound, and finally dragging up to her room to huff oxygen and throw up all night. In the morning she wakes, pants a moment, then tears off for another day of joyous consumption. I shuffle along behind, cautious, snail-like, avoiding hasty movements, head-bending and hills.

Unfortunately, our hotel is on a hill.

Mary and I are vying for the Altitude Intolerance Award, but the difference is that I am doing next to nothing and she is doing everything.

On the final day of our trip I decide, after a paper-thin lunch, to trail Mary for an hour. She's bought a pair of darling Peruvian boots and has decided that she might buy ten more pairs to sell at home—Oh, did I mention that Mary is an entrepreneur?

We zip around the main square together, darting in and out of shops, touching, talking, comparing. She chats up the boot seller, seals the deal, and we make the climb back up to the hotel, Mary dragging a huge bag of boots, and me just barely able to drag a pair of dry, apoplectic lungs. The two-block ascent has me convinced I'm about to flat-line. I slither up to my room, slide under the covers, shiver for an hour (it's not cold) and consider whether I might lift the ban on barfing.

Mary grabs her husband for another sprint to the boot store.

By evening I'm recovered enough to meet my friends for dinner. I order four leaves of lettuce and wash it down with three liters of water, while Mary orders something fascinating and washes it down with wine. We all tuck in for an early evening.

Once I am in my room, I begin to reflect on Mary's health and relative treatment of her threadbare system. Somewhere during my discussion with myself, my inner-bossy-pants begins to dominate. "You know what Mary really ought to do… She ought to stop. Just stop. Stop running, stop talking, stop consuming, stop everything and listen."

I cannot bear Miss Bossy-Pants and threaten to leave if she continues in this manner, but she doesn't hear me.

"She can't expect to hear the answer if she doesn't pause long enough to listen." The bossy one is definitely gaining ground. I've got to do something about her.

"And furthermore, if she doesn't listen in the good times, she will panic in the ill times and never get to the bottom… Blah blah blah, boss boss boss."

I tuck into bed and have a word with myself.

"I don't want to follow these spiraling, negative thoughts. I love Mary. I just want to pray for her."

And so I do. I close my eyes and imagine a huge pair of divine hands and place Mary inside them. I see her wriggling around as the hands attempt to work their magical calming effect. "That's a nice image," I say to myself, and fall instantly, heavily asleep, and do not wake until the sun is well risen the next day.

My husband and I were the first to arrive at breakfast that morning and the table was full of our friends by the time Mary arrived. She told us that she had had a most amazing experience in the night's wee hours.

Unable to sleep, she had tossed and turned for much of the night, dozing some, but mostly ticking off the hours on the clock, 12:00, 1:00, 2:00. Finally at 4:00 she sat up in bed and looked over at a painting that hung next to her bed. It was of a religious figure (saint, angel) with his hands neatly tucked in front of his chest. She stared at the painting for a moment and then, she claims, the figure's hands began to move. She was having a sort of vision. I must interject here that of all the gifts Mary might possess, those of the mystic or visionary would not be the first to spring to mind. The hands in the painting were, she continued, very decidedly moving, and specifically the index fingers of each hand, which unfolded and began to point into one of the corners of her room. She watched these moving fingers for a moment, and then turned toward the corner indicated.

This, I must warn, is where the fantastic grows mystical.

Peering through the darkness, Mary saw the silhouette of a person kneeling in the corner of her room. This figure appeared to be praying, with hands pressed together. She watched for a moment, noting the profile, the hair, the hands, and thought that the figure might be me. After a moment, the apparition (if you will) turned to face her, erasing any doubt. At which point she said that my praying hands drew apart, and with palms facing the floor, moved slowly downward, in a calming gesture.

Mary said that she shed one tear and fell into a sound sleep.

I CONFESS I was shocked, and mightily ashamed, as if a strong wind had blown my skirt above my head to reveal my bossy-under-pants. I should have prayed immediately, prayed longer, not fallen so instantly asleep. Why, I thought to myself, do I ever allow The Bossy One audience? It took me weeks to confess my side of the story.

I have always suspected that there was a greater self than the one that walks this earth, loves sporadically, prides itself in knowing what's best for another and sometimes stumbles into prayer. Each of us has such a grand eternal self. It wouldn't surprise me if these greater selves, stripped of all finite judgment, went walking about at night. It wouldn't shock me to learn that we often visit one another in undiluted prayer.

5
My Dog Tater

I used to get my hair cut by a very wise man in my country neighborhood. He worked out of his home and the floor of his studio was filled with very large, sleeping dogs. I once asked him, "What, among the great wash of humanity that has traveled through this room, have you observed of the human psyche?"

He offered that what troubled him most was its general lack of passion. Most people, he told me, seemed to be slogging through. He didn't expect much, he confessed, just some expression of fond interest, some warm curiosity. One man had a great passion for antique binoculars. He had a collection of them and spoke about them with the robust enthusiasm of a teenager in love, describing each one and how it had come into his life.

His infectious delight, my friend said, was a rare and welcome addition to his day.

We've all known sad souls who, out of supreme frustration, attempt to turn their backs on their passions: the pianist who couldn't achieve the success that he had envisioned and refuses to touch a piano key, the writer who burns all of her writing, the healer who avoids the sick, the minister who shuns the poor. Because, as they see it, the world did not support them, they have decided to deny their gifts and refuse them purchase in their lives. The world is very slow to catch on, it's true. The masses move in inches. It's the individual that has the capacity to soar.

I have a friend, a singer, who has been pounding against the doors of the music world for many years, shuffling forward and lurching backward, as most artists do. She sings as I can only imagine an angel might. Her name is Kate McGarry.

Weary of the daily bouts of professional motion sickness (the broken promises, difficult managers, tyrannical club owners), Kate lately confessed to me that she was considering quitting the music business. She was tired, and longed for a gentler ride.

"I'm not sure I want to be a musician anymore," she confided.

"But Kate," I countered, "you are a musician. You will always be a musician. I'm afraid your gift is an eternal one."

I was certain of this. Do what she would with this life, Kate's was a gift that could not be returned.

I suspect most of us have indulged in this fist-wagging frustration with the heavens. Most have threatened at some point to throw in the towel, the pencil, paintbrush, stethoscope, chisel, guitar. "If you can't support me, if you won't find a place for me in this world," we rattle, "I'll quit!"

I can imagine the heavens looking down on our hysterics with smiling patience.

"Quit what?" they ask. "Quit loving? Can you?"

I knew a young man, a songwriter, who grew so tormented by his thwarted attempts to be successful that he not only refused to write the music that he loved, but declined to give audience to the music that he admired, giving away all of his beloved CDs and saturating himself in the music that he claimed the world wanted, music that he abhorred. He determined to write dreck for the lovers of dreck. Of course he was bound to fail miserably, and be miserable in the attempt.

It's love that propels us to create, not cynicism.

After many years of wrestling with my own frustrations, I have concluded that our gifts are just that, they are gifts. We might possess the power to postpone their use, try and hide from them, but I suspect we only manage to shade ourselves for a time from the intensity of our passions. This love of ours still shines brightly all around, and waits for us with the focused attention of a beloved dog. When we finally step out from under the protection of our denial, our loves will leap and bark and joyously circle us, too long neglected, racing forward and dashing back to us, hurrying us along on our illuminated path.

Who knows, someday we might find ourselves in a place where there is no hypocritical endeavor: where there are none who write because they believe they are clever, who sing to capitalize, who paint to shock, who practice medicine to make money, enter politics to gain power, join the ministry to preach separation.

Perhaps all that this day really requires of us is to step out from under the cover of our resistance, step out and into the warmth of our loves. To say, today I will do this because I love it. I will write what I love, sing what I love, listen to what I love, read what I love, practice what I love, speak what I love.

I will love what there is to love today, and leave the details to a wiser hand.

I WATCHED A documentary once on the lost boys of Sudan. In order to escape death during a brutal civil war, they walked across their county to find refuge in Red Cross camps in Ethiopia. When unrest broke out in that country, they walked again to camps in Kenya. Many died in the process. In these encampments they were given food, shelter and clothing, with the addition of education. After years of heroic struggle to save their lives and the lives of their brothers, after burying so many of their loved ones, after such courageous perseverance, and after finally finding safety, many of them questioned whether they should put an end to their lives—lives that in some cases they had spent ten years of agonizing effort to preserve. While they lingered in camp, they were being kept alive, yes, but to what purpose?

People, it seems, do not like being treated like caged hamsters. But then I suspect neither do hamsters.

Love, these boys had, love was all around them. In order to survive the grueling journey, they had created families, with the older boys taking care of the younger. "All you need is love," the Beatles suggest. I'm not convinced. Love helps us to feel as if we belong, but we need more than love to wake us, drive us through our days.

After the basic needs are met, what is it that moves us on to seek other satisfaction? Is it freedom? I'm not so sure about that. Those who win the lottery and are free to do whatever they please often lose their minds. Look at the children of the fabulously rich.

Retirement can be difficult for so many. Why? The act of winning life's basic necessities, especially when there are others, children for instance, who are benefiting, must help to fill the human need to be necessary, essential to the movement of life. But how does one fill the need when one is not winning bread?

If breadwinning were the purpose of life on earth, than the more bread won, the greater the winner. But this would place Steve Jobs above Jesus. A gross comparison, but the ludicrous is sometimes a good teacher. Neither can we measure necessity by the number of souls dependent on one's providing, for that would make the tyrannical mother of ten more necessary than the childless man who lovingly cares for his ailing father.

High on my top ten list of necessary souls are dead

writers and dogs. How I would have negotiated my life without the writer George MacDonald and my dog Tater, I cannot imagine. I have speculated on what it is the two have in common that inspires such a loving reliance. Perhaps it is their willingness to believe in my better self, no matter how I behave. It is our true friends, our true lovers, who seem to be able to see the God in us, to be able to envision the perfect soul, and are willing to wait, expectant, confident of its ultimate unveiling. They are like my beautiful, potato-shaped yellow Labrador Tater, who when she finds herself on the wrong side of a closed door, will wait with perfect patience for that door to open. While the other dogs that share my life won't let ten seconds go by before they grow impatient and bark (sometimes incessantly), Tater waits like a Quaker, in a state of perfect expectancy, occasionally lifting her front paws in anticipation. The door opens eventually, she knows this. She believes.

I listened to a psychologist on the radio one day. A woman called in to speak of her father who had suffered from mental illness when she was growing up, and on many days hadn't been able to speak to her, let alone provide for her. She was very understanding, very kind about him.

"But," she began to add, when the psychologist completed her thought, "all any of us really wants is to be taken care of."

"Really?" I thought, "Once we are past childhood, don't we want to be able to take care of ourselves?" Those boys in the U.N. camps, they were being taken care of, prisoners are being taken care of, hamsters are taken care of. Surely this man is mistaken.

I suspect we all need to feel a sense of purpose.

Let me look at those around me, those characters whom I have admired, who choose to live and work with the catastrophically poor around the world, teach in the inner city, nurse, diagnose, console, those who stayed up all night to watch my mother sleep the deep sleep of Alzheimer's disease. But, I am not sure those people know their value anymore than any of us. We are probably the last ones to be able to measure our own worth. The good father of five might be judged for his job at British Petroleum, while the criticizing mother of one is valued for her career as a social worker.

We cannot step outside ourselves, and so cannot imagine the effect we have in the world. Being thus blinded, I suggest we leave the judgment to some wiser over-soul, and trust that underneath our oddities is something useful, still in the process of unfolding.

I like to imagine that there is one who, like my dog Tater, watches the door of my soul, one who is content for the time being with the dim light that escapes from around its edges.

The door will open eventually, the full light revealed. I know this.

6

Rising Themes

I meet every Tuesday at 11:00 for an hour with a teacher of Italian conversation. He and I have made a pact to avoid two things: one word of English and the mundane.

When one of us asks, "Che cosa c'e di nuova?" or "What's new?" neither of us is tempted to answer with where we've been, who we've seen, what we're planning for the weekend, but instead to attempt to discover the week's rising theme.

We have both noticed the cyclic rise and return of life themes. These can take the form of lessons, challenges, or the exploration of spiritual principles. They can be as ponderous and longwinded as mourning a loved one and can go on for years and years, or as trifling as an attention to tidiness, lasting only a few days. They can be a month of light study, or a life's worth of struggle.

Recently, in answer to the question "Che cosa c'e di nuova?" I answered that the theme that appeared to be on the rise in my life was detachment. Detachment as the Buddhists view it. Not detachment of feelings, I explained, but an unwillingness to allow my distraught feelings to control my thoughts. "Non si puo aiutare dove va il cuore," I quoted from the I Ching, the book of ancient Chinese philosophy, "Ma soltanto dove va la mente." You cannot help where the heart goes, but only where the mind goes.

I went on to speak of my struggle with the practice of detachment during a recent state election. I had supported a good man's race to retain his seat in congress. He was a soldier who had both served in and questioned the wisdom of the Iraq war. I feared that dirty politicking might make him lose his seat, and my county would lose a very fine legislator.

I explained that the week before I had volunteered to sit at the table in front of the polls at my local municipal building. I arrived, settled in, took several deep breaths, and attempted to be mindful of where my thoughts were taking me. I was feeling both weary of the contentious nature of politics, and grateful that my little polling place had retained its friendly air, when a man walked up. I guessed him to be on the other team, not sure why, just a hunch. Much to my surprise, he sat next to me, having volunteered to sit at the table for the same hours as I had. We began to talk.

He was somewhere in his seventies, of Irish parents, raised in Queens, New York, and had worked hard to become a lawyer. When he was in his twenties (this was during the sixties), he had worked for the campaign of a presidential candidate whose platform was founded on crushing the civil rights movement. He told me that his hard-working Irish parents didn't know what to think of him. He moved to Texas to practice law during a time when that state was executing two hundred people a year. His heart began to crack open. He ended up working for the criminal justice system, defending young men, all of them African American. Then, I take it, his heart broke open completely. He told me that these young men were charged with misdemeanor after misdemeanor until they lost all privileges: driver's license, ability to own a house, hold a job, until there was no hope for them, no possibility of leading a productive life, and then the court would somehow manage to put them away permanently. His face as he told me this was one of perfect compassion. He felt the system was simply designed to remove these young men from society, and I could see that each one of these defendants had blown a little hole through his heart.

We sat together lamenting the injustices of our country's justice system. With less than five percent of the world's population, the U.S. has nearly twenty-five percent of its prisoners. Something is not working. We have more prisoners than China. Something is definitely not working.

He told me that he was a practicing Catholic and was

pro-life, but didn't believe the government should be in-volved in a woman's right to choose, adding that pro-life meant to him not only the rights of those unborn chil-dren, but the preservation of those executed Texans, as well as the one hundred thousand Iraqi civilians killed in a needless war. He told me that most of his friends, many in his parish, didn't see the world from his viewpoint, but that he kept talking to them, and would continue to do so. All of this was said with great gentleness, great kindness toward those who didn't believe as he did, great attention to the needless suffering of humanity. Our time together in front of the polls swept by.

When I left the municipal building that evening, in-stead of the dark premonition I'd been carrying around for weeks (the possibility of my good soldier losing his seat), I was left with the hopeful feeling that comes with the brush with a benevolent soul. "I met an enlightened man today," I told my husband, as we watched the elec-tion results come in. My good soldier lost his election that day.

I have learned that you cannot fool your heart into not caring. It will, it always will. But, you can ask your mind not to follow those thoughts that threaten to spiral downward into despair. Instead, you can feed your mind good, generous thoughts that might lift it, perhaps illu-minate your spirit, and therefore feed your heart.

Detachment, if practiced correctly, would never al-low you to pass over suffering, but will help you to keep your heart open, ready to hold everyone with kindness, even those who do not share your views.

Absolute compassion, the sort that throws you into spiraling despair, without the practice of detachment would be devastating. There is simply too much heart-crushing cruelty in this life.

At our next meeting my Italian-speaking friend asked me whether I really believed that politicians had the power to change the hearts of men.

"That's a loaded question," I answered. "Some of the worst people in power have managed to enlighten through bad example, but so have some of the finest, by good."

I suppose it will always come back to the individual soul.

Enlightenment happens one human at a time, like popcorn. We burst open, one tiny pop, then another pop, then another and another: pop... pop... pop.. pop.. pop, pop, pop-pop-pop... Un umano per volta, ci apriamo improvvisamente, uno pop, e poi un altra pop, poi un altra e un altra, pop-pop-pop-pop-pop-pop-pop!!

7

A Path Revealed

For many years now I have wished to find a way of lifting people's spirits by words. There have been a multitude of times in my life when I have been saved, literally pulled out of despair by words, some spoken, most written. I long to return the favor.

Emerson suggested that one write to the "Unknown Friend." At some point in my early adult years I picked up the pen to apply myself to this task, and I continue to this day.

I would like to say that I always believed that my words would find their audience, that my writings would reach their unknown friends, but I am not blessed with such a sure faith. A gaping, mile-wide flaw in my character is a tendency toward bone-rattling uncertainty.

Though the belief that my life is carefully held in the all-loving hands of a Great Spirit comes quite easily, my faith breaks down when I try and trust that this power intends to help me achieve my goals. Perhaps this is because I can see that my failures have been such grand lessons for me, and I doubt whether disappointment has yet taught me all that I came here to learn.

My respect for the great lesson plan has not kept me from praying for aid in reaching my goals, however, and I have begged the heavens on a daily basis to help me find those who might benefit from my writing.

The difficulty is, the supplication has barely left my lips before I call out the hounds of doubt to chase down the slow rising prayer, circle it, and shake the poor thing by its spindly neck.

This nagging pattern of daily prayer and instant distrust is, I believe, not only weak-willed on my part but disrespectful of the one to whom I pray. I dearly hope to conquer the habit.

When the idea for Listen Well was conceived and on its way to collecting a community of listeners, and as my frustrations with finding a place for my writings were beginning to subside (frustrations that had been building for over twenty years), I experienced a lovely metaphorical moment.

Before I relate this experience, allow me to introduce you to my grandmother, Jane Norton. Jane was an artist all the years of her long life. She dabbled in many different mediums, developing special paints for unusual surfaces. One such phase had her collaborating with the

University of Louisville to come up with a paint that might be used on Plexiglas. Jane was a sort of artist-alchemist. In one of her abstract periods she created a painting on thick parchment, and framed it between two pieces of dense glass. This was one of the few creations in the large Jane Norton collection that my grandmother chose to live with, and the picture hung in a prominent position in her living room. The painting was a gorgeous, cloudlike swirl in gentle pastels, and I would guess that it had hung in her home for over twenty years before she died, at which point the painting came to live with me. By the time of this story the picture had hung in my own home for an equal number of years.

One day, several months after creating Listen Well, the picture, or perhaps my perspective, entirely shifted, and the dreamy swirl of blues and greens suddenly sharpened into a very clear country road traveling down a slight decline, through a spring landscape, and continuing with a curve into an inviting forest. "Ah," I gasped, "I see the path! I see it!"

THIS WASN'T THE first time that I believed I had heard from Jane Norton in connection with my writing. When I was in my twenties and frustrated with the difficulties of finding work in the New York performing arts, my grandmother suggested I try and find an artistic outlet that did not depend on being hired to create. This was sound advice, and I would recommend it to anyone, whether they wish to make a living in the arts or not. Another way of putting this is, find something you love to do, whether it is recognized and supported by the world or not, a passion that will feed your soul in the lean times.

It wasn't until after my grandmother left this world that I began to explore the art of putting words together, and the first thing that I wrote was a play. About nine months into this project, and as I began to polish the first draft, I decided that I needed something better to work with than my old typewriter. It was time I made some sort of pledge to this new direction, and I thought I would do so by springing for a self-correcting machine. I could have searched for a computer but I wasn't prepared to make such a rash commitment.

I found myself in a store on Amsterdam Avenue and 78th Street asking a storeowner whether I might look at one of his fancy typewriters. The man pulled down from his shelves a likely candidate, grabbed a piece of scrap paper near at hand, fed it through the machine, and turned the thing around to face me. The scrap paper had two words written on it. I took in a short breath, and without touching the machine, asked the man to pack it up, I would be taking it with me. He looked mildly surprised, and did as I asked.

When I arrived home with my new typewriter, I called my mother.

"I have a story for you," I told her. "I've just been shopping for a new typewriter and the first machine that was demonstrated to me had a piece of scrap paper fed into it. There were two words written on it. You won't believe this."

"What were they?" she asked.

"Jane Norton." I replied.

"Oh," she answered, "But didn't you realize, this is the anniversary of your grandmother's death?"

It was years before I could throw out that typewriter.

Those hounds of doubt, the ones that have been chasing down my prayers for so many years seem to be slowing down these days. Perhaps, like me, they're aging. Maybe the next time I go off to pray, I'll let them stay at home and sleep.

Reconstructing a Self

8

A Gentle Calling

In my twentieth year I attended a performing arts college as a theater major. After a month or so it was clear to me that the school's curriculum had been designed around the relentless demolition of my youthful self-esteem. I remember one teacher pointing me out to a group of students as an example of one "who would never make it in the profession." "Look at her," he said, "and beware that you don't turn into her." And this because one night among twenty in a series of performances, I had forgotten to carry a coat onstage to indicate that I had walked in from the outside. After two years in this wrecking-ball atmosphere, what self-confidence I had when I arrived had been completely leveled.

One day during the second year of my dismantling,

I entered a grocery store in search of a can of tuna fish and experienced a sudden, raging attack of agoraphobia. Walking through the aisles, the linoleum swam under my feet, the aisles caved in and the muzak seemed to be orchestrated by a madman. I raced for the door, swearing never to enter such a hellish place again.

A day later, I was home, following my mother around the house. I confessed to having had a minor breakdown but I didn't tell her how frightened I was, not wishing to worry us both with fears of future freak-outs and utter, life-long dependence. This respite helped and two weeks later I returned to school to see the year out, but concluded that a third year would annihilate me.

That fall I moved to New York City, to try and find work as an actor. With ninety percent unemployment, the theater might not have been the wisest of choices for someone attempting repairs on a collapsed self-image.

The search for an agent was particularly dehumanizing. I remember waiting in the lobby for a meeting with a prospective manager. The appointment just before mine was for a teenage girl who was accompanied by her mom. The door was cracked and I heard the agent say to the mother, "She's a little on the hefty side. What have you been feeding her?" The mother, apparently unfazed, went on to describe the ratio of carbohydrates to protein that made up the poor thing's diet. Had I mistakenly entered the offices of Bovine Management? I silently tiptoed out the door.

My anxiety in those years in New York caused me dizzying heart palpitations and sleepless nights. When I held up my strengths to my weaknesses, the weaknesses so outweighed the rest of me that I developed a whole new crushing mental malady—self-criticism. I could not come up with a single reason why I should be allowed to occupy a place in the theater, the city, the world for that matter. I began to wish that I might be politely dismissed, as from a class in which I showed a hopeless lack of promise.

One horrible night, I was unable to sleep for the seventh night in a row, and there was a loud party going on in the apartment above. I reached the limits of my despair. Begging, pleading with the heavens to release me from this life, I willingly admitted that I had failed at this thing called living and wanted to go home, follow God around the house.

Around 4:00 a.m., in a brief spasm of self-preservation, I did climb the stairs to the apartment above to ask the revelers to turn down their music. The door opened and I was greeted by a cheerful woman in her underwear, who offered me earplugs and a line of cocaine. I declined both, and returned to my bed.

It was after this night that I began to seriously reflect on the devastation of those two years of art school. I could see that at some point during the dismantlement of my self-esteem, I must have joined forces with the dem-olition crew, started kicking around my own rubble.

I began to watch what I called myself when things weren't going well. If I broke something, feared some-thing or failed at something, I would watch my inner language, particularly the way I addressed myself. Here are some words that I removed from my vocabulary: "stupid," "failure," "loser." Here are some of my alterna-tives: "dear," "love," or just my name, "Margaret," kindly spoken. I began to treat myself more as a good parent might a child, rather than a bully picking on a misfit. "That's ok, dear," I would gently suggest, "you'll know better what to do next time."

This process began for me the slow creeping move-ment toward the reconstruction of a sense of self, one based on the foundation of kindness and belonging, on the understanding that all of those who have been placed on this earth have their place here.

I believe this foundation of kindness has allowed me a glimpse of who I was before I came into this life, and who I might be after I leave this world, of who the spirit is behind this finite personality of mine.

THE SEVENTEENTH CENTURY mystic Emanuel Swe-denborg claimed to have made waking visits to the spir-itual world. One attribute he stressed again and again was the utter transparency of souls in the life eternal. From his numerous journeys, he would describe a place where the words of the mouth and the meditations of the heart were one and the same, where hypocrisy was an impossibility.

As much as I love the idea of a state of existence where there would be no more duplicity, I can see that this is not the state of current earthly conditions. As much as I long for this life to be an all-embracing, empathetic experience of global brotherhood, I can see that for the most part it is not. Swedenborg's visions are extraordinary, precious encounters of divine connection, but they are very rare. Yet, I cannot help but suspect that this world of isolated selves serves some educational purpose.

Since I became involved in the theater in my teens, I have had recurring dreams of playing various roles onstage. These dreams are typically allegories of being unprepared (of stepping on stage without a clue of what I am doing, what my lines are), but some go a bit deeper. Whatever part I am playing, in whichever comedy or drama I have been cast, I can see that the dream is a reflection of my present role in waking life.

As the Bard suggested, that *"All the world's a stage, and all the men and women merely players."* Some roles can be uncomfortable, even though we know that they need to be played: the unpopular parent, unforgiving boss. There will be times when we're asked to be the catalyst for another's change, although we're sure to be perceived as the antagonist. But we are on planet Earth, not yet perfectly, nakedly in love with one another. We still have our separate roles to play.

In a few of my dream productions I have questioned

whether the role that I was being asked to play was necessary to move along the story of the play (a question that I often asked myself as a playwright). "Does this play really need a disappointed bystander?" I might ask. "Is this really necessary to the plot line?"

In other dreams I am making the difficult decision to leave the production, the cast and crew, and find another play, one that is a better fit for me.

In a recent dream, I was having a discussion with the play's director. He turned to me and emphasized a point that he had been trying to make. "Listen Margaret, no matter what role you are playing, no matter what is being asked of your character, you need to make positive choices." I awoke instantly.

Now, this advice is something that is used in the theater by teachers and directors. The thinking being that if you make weak, apathetic choices, if you mumble and lean on the furniture, the audience will not sympathize with you, and you will lose them. You could substitute the word passionate for positive. If you want to run away, leap up and run! If you want to stay and fight, throw your chest out, stand your ground.

The suggestion to make passionate choices reminds me of a story my nephew tells of his experience after a car accident. At a certain point he believed he was speaking with God.

"What are we supposed to do with this life?" he asked of God.

"Just live it," was God's answer.

My dream director would say the same. Accept your role, and live it whole-heartedly.

HERE'S A THOUGHT. What if this earth life, this brief period of time that we spend here, in our separate bodies, in seeming isolation, is quite unique among the experiences offered to us in the long eternal haul? What if, before we come here, we are shown that this particular lifetime is a special, rare opportunity for us, offered to us as if it were a really juicy role in a play?

We would be like actors getting a phone call from an agent, after a successful audition. "They loved you!" chirps the voice over the phone, "They want you. It's a huge opportunity for you. It's a funny, tragic, zany tear-jerker. Perfect cast, big director, it's gonna make you."

"Oh," we think, "I can't wait to sink my teeth into that one," rubbing our hands together.

"Zany, you said?"

"Zany as hell!"

"Some melodrama thrown in?"

"It's loaded with it!"

"Any of those scenes where I get to laugh and cry at the same time? Really show my stuff?"

"Oh, there'll be some gut-wrenching, believe me, you're gonna tear up the scenery."

Then we suddenly grow practical.

"How much are they offering?"

"What?!" the agent yelps, "With a production like this you're asking what it's worth to you?"

"You're right, you're right," we say, apologetic, "what, am I crazy?"

We don't want to lose our agent.

"I'll take it!" we blurt.

The play opens, the reviews are good. It's somewhere in the middle of the run that we grow doubtful. "I wonder if this is really the best play for me. Hmph. Shouldn't I have been cast in some light romantic comedy? Not this thing—this is some kind of a saga. And since when did I start playing the supporting character? I thought I was the romantic lead. I'd better have a word with the director."

At this point it might be wise to take his advice about making positive choices, to believe that there must be good reason why we were cast in our various roles.

Who knows, this may be your only chance to play a childless fifth grade teacher in rural Romania. Might as well play it with passion!

9

Bob and Company

There is a handy tool of the Buddhist trade that suggests that when one is meditating and stuff pops up, stuff we wish hadn't popped up just when we were trying to empty our minds of that sort of stuff, it is useful to look at this stuff and name it. "Oh," you might say, "there's frustration," or perhaps "Oh, lookee there, uh-huh, insecurity."

The idea is that naming it will help you to detach from this visitor (and the invasion of your meditative privacy), and simply watch with a passive eye as these feelings—anger, fear, resentment—get bored with your not paying them any attention and toddle off.

I have such a visitor that haunts me on my morning walk through the woods. I can be noodling along, dreamy, feeling like the most fortunate being on the earth, when a nasty thought arises, like a creepy guy popping out from behind a tree. My first reaction is to shudder and grow irritated, and wonder why he's visiting me in this of all places, in my lovely woods.

The thoughts that typically make surprise attacks on my psyche are of the "why bother" variety, those feelings that try and convince me that nothing will ever come of any idea that I ever manage to dream up, and so why not give up now, save myself the anguish. I have wondered what to name this frequent visitor. No single word seems to encompass all that this feeling suggests, and so I have decided to name him Bob. No associative reason for this, it's just a name.

Bob likes to show up at the most inconvenient times: at the birth of a new idea, the moment I sit down to write, as I reach for the phone. He delivers the same message, always. The language might be varied, but the message is the same. "Give up now," he warns, "don't get too attached to the idea, you're headed for heartache. Remember heartache? Ouchy."

Bob, it seems, has a little alarm next to his bed. Whenever I have a new idea, one over which I am feeling a degree of enthusiasm, the bell goes off next to Bob's head. He doesn't waste any time, he leaps out of bed, throws on some clothes and dashes over to see what he can do to discourage me. If the idea is one that requires some perseverance, some confident resolve, Bob starts plotting his attack. The cynical approach is his favorite.

Let's say, for instance, I decide that I would like to move from writing plays to writing nonfiction.

"Puh," he snorts, "you?"

And, let's say that I would like to collect some stories on faith.

"Hold on," warns Bob. "Back up a minute," he sneers. "You?"

And let's say I imagine that eventually I might be able to find an audience for these stories.

Bob's in a sarcastic lather by now. "And how big are your britches, huh?" he scorns. "Last I looked you were a nobody."

Now he has my attention.

"Everybody's a nobody before they are a somebody," I counter.

Bob's got me now. He loves the somebody/nobody argument. Maybe he can squash the idea before it sends down the tiniest root.

"What if everybody who thought they were a nobody stopped at nobody and never tried to be somebody?" I sputter.

I'm hooked. Bob's got me where he wants me.

"Oh, so you want to be a somebody, do you?" Bob is so sneaky.

"Damn!" I shiver, now he's going to pull out the bloated ego warning, the one that equates all ambition with narcissism.

"There wouldn't be a single book to read if writers had no aspiration." I'm starting to yelp. "There wouldn't be any improvement in the world if people with fine ideas didn't have goals." I look around to see if anyone can overhear us.

Bob has me now.

I see him planning his final, lethal blow.

"But those are winning people, you're talking about, dear." (Bob can be so condescending.) "Those are people who win. W.I.N." (Bob likes to spell things out.) He leans in, his hot breath directly in my ear. "That doesn't happen to you, does it?"

I stare at him, feet shuffling, panting, wondering what that Buddhist advice was that I had read about, that thing about naming.

"Bob," I suddenly spurt, "I didn't recognize you at first. So it's Bob again. Bob, B.O.B." (I give him a little taste of his own medicine.) "Bob... Bob, Bob, Bob, you know what you are? You are a big, unattractive liar."

"Really?" he counters, unflinching, "Let's take a look at your history."

Now, I know better than to take him up on this offer. It won't go well. We'll be wallowing in resentment before we know it. Bad idea.

No, no, no, it's like that staring game when you were a kid. You try and stare at the other kid until he blinks. You stare and you stare. Your eyes are beginning to dry up. Your eyes are totally drying up, they're starting to feel like little raisins inside their sockets. Everything is drying up, all of your good ideas, all of your enthusiasm, all of your chutzpah. It's up to you to do something. "This is stupid," you think. "Why am I even engaged in this game?" you ask yourself. "It's pointless."

You blink. Turn your head. Take a deep breath, and walk on.

I have to say that Bob's not looking so robust lately; he's lost a lot of weight. If he gets any punier, I'll be able to knock him over with a pointed glance. What a day that will be. I'll level him with look, flatten him with a flick of the eyes. What a sweet day that will be.

IN THE MEANTIME I practice my remedial exercises of saying "yes" to things. It's challenging but very much worth it.

My husband and I were invited to dinner with friends this past New Year's Eve and, having railed against the holiday for so many years—citing its empty promises for a good time, the lateness, the drunkenness—I politely declined. I held out for weeks with this crusty attitude, until my husband reasoned with me. "Couldn't you look at it differently?" he suggested, "it's really just dinner with friends, and you love your friends."

"You're right," I answered, and turned to face one of my oldest, stick-in-the-mud positions.

I did go out that night and enjoyed myself immensely, discovering that I was capable of staying up past midnight, the sidewalks weren't littered with boozing sponge-heads, and the act of ringing in the first of January with friends really does feel as though it could bring a blessing to the coming year.

At some point several years ago, I decided that it

might be prudent to search out and cull those strident rigidities that keep me from living a life of joy. I might at least attempt to be more watchful. I could start by sniffing around my tendencies to say never:

"No, no, I don't do that, it doesn't suit me; I'm not creative, you see. Nope, no, I'm not political; I never go out after nine; I just don't answer those calls; I'm not religious; I don't care for those types; I have no desire to travel there; that doesn't look good on me, nope, and nor does he. Nope, no, I don't eat that, read that, watch that, listen to that, like that, no, never."

The problem is, these niggling negatives so crowd the mind, as if a bunch of loudmouths were pushing into a small cottage. In the congested space that remains, we gasp as these noisy, disapproving windbags suck out all of the air. I wrestle with this belching gang of blowhards often, and I would dearly love to send them on their way. Then why don't I, you might ask? Perhaps I lack the courage to live without them. My cottage would feel so empty. And, anybody might move in!

The experience of New Year's Eve, though, raises the possibility that each isolating negative that we're willing to face and expel allows that much more fresh joy to squeeze into our cottages. But, it takes courage to confront this agitated gang of security guards, and courage requires a certain degree of trust.

Trust in what, you ask? Whatever fills the empty space left from the absent, nagging opposition. Whatever it is that seems to arrive when you need it: new friends, new ideas, new ventures.

Unfortunately, the more crowded our cottages, the less likely we are to give room to anything new. *"A small-minded man weighs what can hinder him,"* states my little book of Hindu wisdom, *"and fearful, dares not set to work."* If we could anticipate the parade of obstacles that march toward us, would we embark on any endeavor?

The trick is, how are we to invite these noble visitors, the ones we call inspiration, enthusiasm, passion, surprise—how are we to entertain these grand guests in the close cottages of our minds? How, with that horde of brawling gasbags in there, stinking up the joint?

Here is my answer. I'm afraid it is my only answer, and this, after years of wrestling, after confronting and banishing hundreds of misgivings, after kicking the noisy yellow-bellies out one door, only to watch them race in another, madder than ever. My answer: ask.

Don't worry about the state of the cottage, just ask. Those fatheads inside won't help you clean up, you can bank on that, they will complain and warn, tell you that you're not being realistic. They love that word, realistic. "How can you invite those guys in here?" they shout, "look at this place, be realistic!"

"But I can't breathe in here for all of this realism!" you reply.

Just ask.

Have you ever invited someone into your home and that person notices the very thing that you most love, even seems to admire it for the same reasons you do? "That little glass bird on your windowsill, look how it catches the light! This lumpy, old dog, is she as much of an angel as she appears? This idea that you mentioned, I think it is a good one, you should work toward it."

"Come in. Come in," you might say, "I have no better place to offer. You'll have to ignore the lousy company, step over their clutter, but I know you will find what it is I love. And, I know it will be as precious to you as it is to me. Come in, please."

You might notice the windbags clamming up and shuffling their feet. One of the them might put a few things in his carry-on bag, another might slip out the door. This could cause another to follow and another. The next thing you'll notice is the silence, which will allow you to hear the one voice remaining. The one that says, "Why not try."

10

The Next Small Truth

If God were a fretter, and I don't pretend to know whether or not this is true, I assume that the thing that would keep him up at night would be the question of what his children will be bringing back when they come home from this life. Like parents who send their twelve-year-old off to camp, there is the hope that the child will learn more than how to torture bugs, short-sheet beds and smoke cigarettes.

Most people would probably agree that when we cross through the Great Door and back to our old home, the only thing that we will be able to carry with us is the person we have become. All else will be left behind: earthly accomplishments, awards, fame, piles of stuff, successes, failures, mortgages, debts, all of the stuff of life that we have stirred up, even our relationships. We pass through that door alone.

Imagine. We can shove nothing else into our little backpack, nothing, but this person that we have grown into.

I confess I find the notion perfectly exhilarating.

Some hint of what this might look like might be understood by studying our lives. It is quite impossible to divide our thoughts, our feelings, our attitudes from the circumstances of our lives. One could say that our lives perfectly describe our selves. We are made of the same airborne stuff as our earth, our galaxy. Our temperaments are like the wind: sometimes stirring, sometimes placid, occasionally raging, rarely perfectly still. By looking at the effect the soul's current of air has had on the surrounding stuff of life, we understand ourselves.

"*By their fruits ye shall know them*," Jesus explains.

WHEN I WAS thirty-three I picked up the pen for the first time. Before this time I seemed to be content with reading. Plays were the first things that I chose to write and I occupied myself with this effort for over twelve years. Perhaps because I had come to the profession at a fairly late age, I never sent a play out without numerous apologies for not knowing what I was doing and assurances of gratefully handing over any ownership of opinion at the first rehearsal. You can imagine that this attitude attracted every bossy-pants in the business. Like honey to a bear, my gooey insecurity was irresistible to the manipulative, and it was nearly impossible for me to find a director whom I could call a true partner. As a result, most of my experiences as a writer in the theater were painful power struggles. The philosopher Rudolf Steiner suggests that our immaturities seek pain. I think he's right.

LATELY I'VE BEEN trying to wrap my mind around the idea that at any moment one's trajectory can shift, and quite another person can come into being. As if we were all great sailing vessels in the open sea, the potential for a storm to blow up and knock us off course is always there. Our ships are rather cumbersome, and it takes a while to change direction, but we can and do change, and this new direction often leads us somewhere quite wonderful.

My yoga teacher, at some point in every class, asks her students to put their hands together in prayer position over their hearts and set an intention for the day. I'm never quite sure what to intend. If my own intention is anything short of God's intention for me, in other words, if it would send me off in a direction that would not lead somewhere good, then I would hope to be kept from following it.

At some point while writing plays I wished to be more confident so that the bullying I was experiencing would cease. I knew that I could not muscle myself into a state of confidence, that a healthy sense of confidence cannot be forced. I felt my only hope was to pray for confidence to be given to me. Or, I should say, pray for confidence to grow in me, since a sudden onset of confidence would look much more like arrogance.

LOOKING BACK, IT is clear to me that my lack of confidence caused a series of small tempests to blow up in my life, most often in the form of some sort of humiliation, and each one caused me to shift my direction slightly. Miraculously, with each new tack, I seemed to come a tiny bit nearer to the person that I wished to become, the one I would be most willing to take with me through the Great Door. It's still summer around here, though, and I presume there will be many more squalls in my sails.

I MET A woman the other day who told me that her life had been a series of humiliations. Had I known her better I might have sung out, "Oh, good for you!"

The word "embarrass" originally meant to impede or hinder. A defending army might "embarrass" an invading one from gaining ground. The same could apply to our invading egos. If we did not suffer embarrassment of some sort, would we not be tempted to march out and take over all of the surrounding territories, with troops of hard-boiled hubristic attitudes raping and pillaging the gentler natures of our neighbors?

This personality, the rampant egocentric, the proverbial horse's ass, the type that insists on adding their names to everything they touch, cannot be made to see the absurdity of their self-serving, aggrandizing arrogance. And, most of us, at some point in our lives, have been these people.

The good news is that a fine peppering of self-centeredness is quite healthy for the young. But, the better news is, if this natural conceit hasn't suffered the kindness of humiliation, been tempered by embarrassment over the years, it will wear an invitation that will beg for humiliation, like a "kick me" sign taped to one's backside. Arrogance sends out a pheromone attracting all of the ridicule within miles.

We must be willing to be small or risk being made to feel small.

"*There shall be no success to the man who is not willing to begin small,*" writes George MacDonald. "*Small is strong, for it only can grow strong. Big at the outset is bloated and weak. There are thousands willing to do great things for one willing to do a small thing but there never was any truly great thing that did not begin small.*"

We have all been exposed to the bloated and weak. They seem to gravitate to positions of power and, when released into the protective arena of spiritual authority, they can be quite dangerous. Beware the one who presumes a closer connection to the divine than your own. The great ones never do.

Many of our grandest teachers, Jesus, the Buddha, Socrates, Epictetus appear never to have picked up the pen, never to have put their names to any writing. They were focused on lifting the hearts of those around them. Content with the present company, for the present moment, they simply sought to uncover the day's truth.

When an interviewer attempts to paint the Dalai Lama as something grand, a soul with a mighty preordained purpose, his response is typically, "I am a monk, a simple monk."

I have come to revere this willingness to be small more than any other human quality. Please don't confuse this attribute with its false mask: the puny stepped on, trampled down, insecurity. Never that. No, I am speaking of confident, clearheaded humility, the kind that looks you in the eye, cares about what you think, who you might be, what potential goodness you offer the world. The kind that listens, that does not need to see its name on anything, does not expect to be honored, remembered or praised, and wishes to leave behind no mark but the effects of kindness.

Indeed I wonder whether it might be nice to create a church of kindness.

I attended a Quaker memorial for a friend's husband at a local meetinghouse recently. This man had been born to a scholarly couple and had carried on the family legacy. After attending both Harvard and Oxford, he became a professor of American literature in a private liberal arts college, where he taught until his midfifties, when he was diagnosed with cancer. He was quite unique among the college's faculty, not only because of his education, but as a member of two minorities: he was both African American and gay.

If you have never been to a Quaker memorial, allow me to paint the scene: the attendees sit in silence until, one at a time, they are moved to speak. Each will stand and tell a story, some anecdote having to do with the person whom they have come to memorialize. I did not know this man well, but knew his husband, (I love being able to say that) and so kept my seat and listened.

The brush strokes of various memories filled in the painting of this man's life. They also strengthened a premise that I have been turning around in my mind for many years, which is that our impression of a man's character is essentially made up of small moments of either kindness or unkindness. And, most of us will prefer, unless the person possessed absolutely no capacity for kindness, to focus on those moments when we were touched by the person's thoughtfulness. And, interestingly, most of these kindhearted acts appear on the surface to be very small.

Many of the kindnesses that were spoken of at the memorial were moments when the person on the receiving end had been feeling isolated, and was made to feel included. There was the student who had been a freshman when she met him, and quite sexually confused at the time. She was made to feel that she fit in, whatever her present or future choices. There was the woman who was made to feel elegant when she identified herself as being quite invisible. There was the young professor, one of three African American teachers among a faculty of three hundred, who was taken under this man's wing, and made to feel as if she belonged.

Several times this man encouraged the person relating the story to speak out, to tell his truth, not to fear being further isolated if he expressed himself. Thirty or so people stood up to tell their stories that day, and all spoke of these moments of connection. None of them wasted more than a moment speaking about this man's grand education, his tenured professorship, or the books he had written.

I don't recall my friend portraying his husband as a man who performed extraordinary acts of kindness. He never spoke of him as unkind, but neither did he picture a man whose principal focus in life was the spreading of thoughtful gestures throughout the community. He was a human, having a human life. He was like all of us.

Apparently this humble view of this man's life accords with accounts from the other side of the grave. Not that I have been there, mind you, but I am a connoisseur of the reports from those who claim to have visited through near death experiences.

According to thousands of stories from the beginning of recorded history, when near death experiencers go very deeply into their adventures on the other side, they will often have a life review. These are described as interactive, three-dimensional movies of the person's life, complete with feelings. One not only experiences one's own feelings but the feelings of the others in the scene as well, those who are affected by one's behavior or words, with or without one's knowledge.

To relieve any trepidation one might have about this part of the process of entering the next world, it appears from most accounts that there is in attendance a being of pure love who guides the observer toward forgiveness, toward compassion for the self.

During these reviews the person witnesses those moments when they touched another person in a positive way, lifted them. Most often these are very small gestures: brief encounters, a smile, one word of encouragement said at the right time, a hand held out, a note written.

I read an account from one man who observed with some consternation during his review that it had skipped over all of the awards that he had won as a child, and seemed not to concern itself with the name he had managed to achieve for himself as an artist. This was met with gentle laughter from his attending spirit.

I can see from my own life that the small kindnesses shown me have made a great deal of difference to the quality of my days, and I would go so far as to say, much more of a difference than any of my achievements.

YES, I THINK it might be time to found a new religion, one based solely on kindness.

Like most churches, there will be unbelievers in the

congregation, members who show up for coffee hour. That's fine. They're very welcome. Many might feel uncomfortable with the first and only tenet, but we welcome those guys too.

The location and hours for worship will be rather slippery.

"Did you go to church today?" one might ask.

"Yes."

"Where did you go?"

"I went to the Kroger at the corner of Grape and Vine Streets."

"Did you see anyone we know?"

"Yes, that little man who bags at 13. The one with the funny legs."

"Oh yes, a fine member of the parish. Did the service last long?"

"No, just two minutes, but I'm very glad I went. He said something that has me thinking."

Ours will be a most unusual church/synagogue/mosque/stone circle arrangement.

The only plate passed will have food on it.

"Did you receive the Holy Sacrament today?" a parishioner might ask of another.

"No, but I plan on it tonight. We're having beanie-weenies with the kids."

One wouldn't have to be literate to read scripture, just cognizant, as the sacred text would only be two words long, and most of us could memorize it: "Be kind."

"Did you go to church today?"

"Yes I did."

"Where?"

"The drycleaners out on highway 33. The owner's old dog is dying. We had a good cry together."

II

The Road to Longsuffering

I sat on the beach this past summer with my niece Sarah (sage beyond her twenty-five years), as she described the amorous activities of some of her female peers. She told me that they were often furious with their male partners over slight gaffes made in all innocence.

"He called me after six o'clock to have dinner with him at eight." one might say.

"I could hardly speak to him all night, I was so incensed."

"But, had you told him previously what the rule was?" Sarah responds.

"Well, no. But he should know better," they will answer.

Sarah says that she feels sorry for the young men, so

often blindsided by their girlfriends' silent fury, without a clue to what their transgressions might have been.

"All of this could have been avoided with a simple conversation," Sarah laments.

"Could you make sure and call me before six if you want to make plans for dinner,' might be an example. 'Otherwise I assume that you are busy.' Just a simple conversation," she sighs.

"And the beat goes on…" I groan.

The two of us pause to reflect upon this age-old dilemma, the same old waves lapping at the ancient shore.

"You remind me," I interrupt our reverie, "that for some time I've been meaning to write a piece on the difference between patience and longsuffering."

There is a line between admirable patience and miserable longsuffering, a slippery spot that I suspect many of us dance around almost daily. It is clear that Sarah's friends have leapt over this line, and are well on their way down the road of longsuffering when they find themselves tight-lipped and fuming at the dinner table, as their male counterparts sit across from them, peeking nervously from out their doghouse doors.

Most of us have at some point in our lives employed the excuse of assumed proper behavior to propel us down the road of longsuffering:

"No one in my family ever helps me in the kitchen," one might say.

"But have you ever asked them to help?" another might counter.

"They can see that I'm slaving away in there, isn't that enough?"

"Apparently not."

We know that we've crossed the line when we grow so irritated that we explode. The sudden discharge indicates that we have stepped over the opportunity for speaking gently, most likely repeatedly, and now step onto the landmine of temper, (a trap that we have laid for ourselves, by the way) and what comes out of us is not nearly so helpful as what might have been released earlier.

At this point we are laboring under the misguided belief that we have lost the chance to speak gently, that we passed that peaceful place long ago.

If you find yourself dragging your feet down the dreary road of longsuffering, stepping around landmines, lamenting your lost opportunity to speak with kindness, I suggest that you stop, take a look around, make sure that no one is watching, throw your head back and holler to the heavens, "Please help me to find that place again, that gentle place again, please."

I will stop here, for I don't wish to travel more deeply into these psychological woods. I merely bring up the example as a platform from which to dive into a less obvious hypothesis, one that requires a little more explanation.

I have for most of my life operated under the belief that my life's journey, and more importantly my thoughts, are carefully followed by the heavens. Please feel free to substitute any word you wish here: God, my guardian angel, guiding spirit. The point I wish to make is that we may not be entirely alone inside our heads, and any obsessive, overworked, nagging complaint that we might inwardly express like "why doesn't anyone but me put the breakfast dishes away?" might be heard by those that care for us from the spiritual world as often as it is repeated in our own thinking. I find this idea rather sobering. It suggests that when I choose not to speak, but rather to circle around a nagging inner complaint, in stony silence, my poor guardian angel, for instance, is forced to listen. Think of it.

The remarkable thing is, I feel quite loved by this guiding presence, no matter how much I complain about things that are within my own power to change, often "with a simple conversation," as Sarah suggests.

I don't believe that we were sent into this world for longsuffering. In fact when we cross over and into the next world, the first thing out of the mouths of those who watched over our lives is likely to be, "Why...? Why didn't you speak? Why, when you were given every opening, why didn't you simply speak?"

I try and imagine this end-of-life reaction when I find myself huffing and puffing on a mad, tight-lipped-junket along the road of longsuffering. I imagine myself hunting for a rest area, one with a comfortable bench and nice view of my life, and perhaps one with an angel sitting on it.

"Have a seat, Margaret." The being will pat the bench next to him, moving aside a great wing.

I sit.

"Now tell me," asks the angel, "what brings you here?"

"Blah-blah-blah-blah," I begin to explain, "and I just can't… I'm afraid I've lost the … the place where I might have… spoken."

"Mmm," the angel ruminates, "There's a turn just ahead."

"A turn?" I repeat.

"Yes," the angel continues, "a different road from this one. If you take it, it will lead you to a peaceful little hollow with the most beautiful acoustics."

"Oh." I reply, hopeful.

"A better spot than the one you feel you have lost, where even the softest whisper can be heard. Your voice, I assure you, will be clear as glass and perfectly under-stood. Go there now and speak."

I begin to move.

"Oh, and there's something more." The angel stops me.

"Yes?" I turn to him.

"You will meet an old friend there."

"Will I?"

"Yes, you'll recognize her. Her name is Patience."

I thank him kindly and walk on.

OF COURSE THE answer to how and when to speak must be weighed carefully.

Several years ago I hired a woman to help me with a

garden project, and it went so swimmingly well that I recommended her around the hood. To abbreviate the story, none of my neighbors had the same jubilant response to working with her, and I received some rather irritated phone calls on the subject. I did feel a bit guilty, but finally concluded that, after all, this woman wasn't mine. By that I mean she was her own person, and not mine to defend, apologize for, counter with praise. The fact is each of us will behave differently with each new encounter, and although there are some temperaments that generally don't mix well with anyone, when paired with certain humors they will act in striking harmony.

I try to be aware of my not owning another in my dealings with everyone these days, both in action and thought. If I am concerned about someone, especially if I feel I know what that person should do to help himself or herself, I will repeat, "He is not mine. She is not mine."

No one belongs to another. Even children are only on loan, to be carried for a time and set back on their feet. I have a friend who tells me that she realizes that at some point she must be willing to "divorce" her children in order to help them to be independent. This is an almost herculean act of bravery on the part of a parent, to stand by while a child falls and fails, but it must eventually be performed, or the child will never find his footing, never find her balance. If the parent won't do this, the child must rip himself away, and that is usually less desirable. If neither will cut the cord, fate will step in and cause the tear. No one wants this; it's usually very ouchy.

It's always easier to see a lesson when it is headed in a

friend's direction than when it's headed your own way. It's equally clear which lessons continue to return and return because the person has not learned from them.

Some friends will try and point out the obvious, try and describe what they are seeing, and others will leave the friend to figure it out on their own. I imagine there is a point of perfect balance between brutal honesty and detached apathy. I have never managed to stay there for very long, but I know it when I find it in others, and gravitate toward those who can be both honest with me and healthily detached.

I do believe that, whether or not we are able to listen to our friends, ultimately it is God who changes us. "God is working his purpose out," as the old hymn goes, and all lessons are divinely gifted. If we are lucky, we have those around us who are willing to describe to us what we are unwilling to see ourselves, but in the end it is God who hands us the lessons and God who helps us to learn them.

This has led me to the conclusion that it is God with whom I should speak first when I am concerned about a friend.

I hope it isn't just a habit of mine to have inner dialogues with people about what they might do to improve their situations. I have mentioned before that I have an inner bossy pants, a rather strident character that is inclined to one-sided, inner conversations that begin with: "You know what you ought to do? You ought to... blah-blah-blah..."

At some point, after the boss has been released, but

before the obsessive guy with the megaphone starts barking, I try and remind myself to whom the other belongs. "Oh, that's right, he isn't mine, is he? He's yours." I say, as I turn to face the heavens.

There are moments when I almost feel the tug of this truth, as if two hands were gently placed on my cheeks, guiding my focus in this better direction.

If I am sincere in this transference of concern, and ask only that this person be helped in their struggles, not by following my directions, but by listening to their own higher guidance, I can sometimes be of use. If I honestly wish to be of service to this better angel of the friend's nature, I will be moved to speak when the time is right, and speak gently.

In my early twenties I had a friend for whom I acted as a sounding board. I believed that my utter silence would be beneficial when she began telling me her problems with her live-in boyfriend. As the months wore on, I heard more and more of the embarrassing details of her relationship with this young man. They were both sleeping around on each other, often with the other's good friends, and hurting each other terribly. I never said a word, just listened.

I would, however, go home to my new husband and vent about the day's discoveries. Adding, "If you ever dare to treat me as these two treat each other, I will walk out that door and never look back." Yet still I went back for more, and still I did not speak, and still I brought my reaction home to my marriage.

Eventually I got a call from this friend who said that her boyfriend had asked her to marry him and she had agreed. Apparently they were looking into purchasing health insurance and discovered that their policy would be cheaper if they were married.

"How romantic," I thought to myself, but still I did not speak.

"You are my first call," she told me, "I know how much you love being married."

"Oh," I thought to myself, "I can think of so many juicy responses to that statement, I hardly know which to choose..." But still, I didn't choose, I didn't speak.

Eventually our friendship fell apart. It had to. One of us wasn't being honest. By my silence, I was practicing perfect complicity. I might as well have cheered them on with whistles and pompoms.

"*Better to be a nettle in the side of your friend than his echo,*" writes Emerson.

You might ask why I never spoke my truth to this friend. At the time I thought her too fragile to hear it, and mistakenly believed I could prop up her delicate psyche with my silence. I thought she was mine to hold up.

As I age, I am more drawn to those who speak honestly to me. No matter how bitter the pill, no matter how long it takes to work, I do want this medicine. Give me your truth and allow me to determine whether it is the right remedy for me. Time will reveal its efficacy.

I would rather hear a truth from a friend, and adjust

my behavior accordingly, than meet the reactions of cold consequence which could be much more harsh.

Maybe it's time to turn that old line from the prayer book around to read, "Speak now and try never to hold your peace." Speak if you must, absolutely. Speak and then step back. Give room. They are God's to teach, God's to hold, God's to heal.

12

Mood Birds

I've been attempting to uproot a longstanding fear. When I was young, I loved to travel, but in my late twenties I wrestled with sleep issues (a period in my life that my husband refers to as the insomnia plague), and I grew fearful of not being able to drop off to sleep, especially when I was away from my own beddy-bye.

Not wishing to give up on travel altogether, I developed various methods of fooling myself. One was the banning of all talk of travel anywhere near bedtime. I discovered that the nearer I came to tucking in, the scarier grew the idea of beds in foreign places. My family and friends were soon trained never to mention the subject of leaving home anywhere near sunset unless they were ready to suffer my gray, groaning moods.

I continued to leave the nest on occasion but not without some major ducking and dodging during the time leading up to the trip, with a full-blown, oily depression the day before departure, and a final mournful slide out the door, sure that my cats and dogs were plotting suicide over my departure.

At some point several months ago, I concluded that my policy of avoidance of all talk of travel before bedtime was a big fat failure, and I needed to find a different strategy.

THE CATHOLIC WRITER and teacher Richard Rohr has some sage advice about the development of character. It goes like this...

> *Watch your thoughts, they become words.*
> *Watch your words they become actions.*
> *Watch your actions they become habits.*
> *Watch your habits they become character.*
> *Watch your character it will become your destiny.*

My fear of leaving home had certainly reached the character phase. My only hope, according to this recipe, was to go back to the beginning: to work on my thoughts.

As fate would have it, my husband was planning to attend a meeting in Guatemala and asked whether I might consider flying down to join him afterward for a trip around the country. Here was a juicy opportunity to change my thinking. Guatemala is ripe with bad press to dampen the most seasoned traveler's enthusiasm: stories of kidnapping and firearms, all night barfing and insidious insects. But, I reasoned, all of these things can be enjoyed in our own country with the number of guns per square mile easily squared. Clearly I could not logically talk myself into this trip by comparing the two countries' relative safety. My only hope was to nip the first hint of negative thinking in the bud before it took hold of me.

Wait, let me back up. I had first to ask the heavens for help. I had to let the peeps upstairs know that I was ready to let go of something, and ask whether they might help me. The years have convinced me that I am a coproduction, not a one-man show. I could not hope to effect permanent change without prayer.

I've found that a negative thought can be sensed before it reaches the mind, as if it gave off a foul odor. Once I catch a whiff of a mean-ass thought, my best hope is to throw up a screen, plunge the nasty thing in a fog of positivity, so that it isn't able to find me.

At first it was just smoke and mirrors. "I can't wait to get to Guatemala!" I would yelp inwardly. "I love traveling in Latin America!" Both thoughts are true, by the way. I do love Latin America, and I do love to visit foreign places.

Unfortunately, these thoughts aren't the first to spring to mind when facing the idea of leaving home. These are more like: "I wonder if they have beds in Guatemala?" or "I hope they have friendly psychiatric care. If I don't sleep for a week I'm sure to be hospitalized."

I decided to head off these thoughts with my strategy of unbridled enthusiasm.

"I am sooooo looking forward to flying down to Central America!" I would bellow to myself "And, I get to do it alone!" Another thing that I loved when I was young was the feeling of freedom when boarding a plane on my own, as if the world were opening up to me in the most delicious way. "Hooray for airplanes full of strangers!" I silently squealed.

I had plenty of time to anticipate this trip, nearly half a year, with lots of opportunities to implement my new method of positive thought. Eventually I began to believe myself, because I was voicing the truth behind my fears with such passion that the truth finally shoved my fears aside to get at me. We embraced like long lost lovers.

The closer the date of travel, the more eager I grew about going on the trip. The day before I was to leave home was spent in happy anticipation, and the next morning I kissed the house pets and skipped out the door.

The trip to Guatemala was gorgeous, but somehow I knew it would be. It was graced with peaceful slumber and rich days, and curiously empty of kidnapping insects carrying chemical weapons.

I understand that I am outlining a rather simplistic policy: just replace the negative thought with the positive. I do know how difficult this can be. It feels so awkward at first, as if you were being told that your walk is all wrong, with the suggestion that you land first on your great toe, roll your foot backwards, and push off from your heel. Impossible.

"But I've been walking this way for a quarter of a century" you might protest. "I've made it this far." "True, true," would be the answer, "but imagine how far you might travel without the burden of fear."

If we could see with our eyes the power of our willingness to change mixed with our prayers and the careful attention to our thoughts, I believe its potential would astound us.

THIS METHOD FOR the deconstruction of a longstanding anxiety can work for the sudden appearance of a vile mood as well.

Moods are like birds, some are light, no more that a few ounces, downy, sweet-voiced, some are blue-black with loud, rasping voices, others are flightless and dense with great, scratchy feet. Some ascend, kite, some float, glide, others land with a vicious thud. I had one such mood descend recently upon the tender ground of my soul. It was pterodactyl in size, with a twenty-foot wing-spread and barbed wire claws. It landed with such heaviness that I feared I would never be able to drag myself out from beneath its bulk.

It appeared one day during the rehearsal period of a production of one of my plays. The director and actors had been working on the play for three weeks or so and the play was coming joyfully to life. Every aspect of the production appeared to be on solid, happy ground. It was the evening of the final dress rehearsal, and the audience was to arrive the next day, when the great lumbering beast arrived. Suddenly I was faced with a mood so dismal and cynical that it threatened to smother every ounce of my hard-earned confidence. All I had worked for appeared to be a pathetic waste: the years of preparation in writing and rewriting, the good work of the director, the enthusiasm and talent of the ensemble. What seemed to me a worthy script was suddenly shamefully trite. What had seemed comical was not, what had felt meaningful was empty. I was horribly embarrassed to have involved my friends in such a dead end effort. Everything looked worthless and stupid and all I wanted to do was crawl away unnoticed and not have to face the next day.

I watched the rehearsal with utter dread of the coming public performance, left the theater in abject despair, and made a mad dash for my bed, but couldn't begin to turn off my negative, spiraling thinking. I snuck downstairs to confess to Matt that I had gone to the dark side. "I hate everything," I told him, "everything about this pitiable play. It's as if my eye were jaundiced. I can't see anything outside my dreary, critical perspective." He did his best to console me, but I was a difficult case.

The next morning I took my daily walk with the dogs in the woods. I headed down to the stream where I typically stop to watch the light play on the water. I had been praying all the while that I might have this black mood lifted from me, feeling sure that it wasn't within my power to lift the thing myself. It had swooped in with such spirit-crushing ferocity that I felt entirely unprepared to fight it off. "Help me," I begged. "My vision has been poisoned. Please lift this darkness from me."

At which point something extraordinary happened. I was staring out at the water, watching the daylight play in the rippling current. There were no clouds in the sky and the reflection was a soft white with silver trimmings. I watched the delicate play of sparkle on the surface of the water for a moment, when the scene before me began to take on an otherworldly quality. The reflection began to grow much, much brighter and at the same time its color was shifting to a brilliant yellow. The color and brilliance grew and grew in intensity, ten, fifty times brighter, until it seemed as if the sun were about to burst through and rise up out of the water. I was tempted to avert my eyes, the light was so very intense, but I felt it was important that I not look away. This might be some sort of curative offering, as if the light were sent as a balm to heal to my vision. The words that came to my mind were, "I am having my mind washed clean." I stood, transfixed, for approximately twenty seconds before the light began to diminish and return to its original display of gentle tones. I stood a while longer, breathless.

The great, terrifying mood-bird had been lifted and I was myself again. Hallelujah.

IN LOOKING BACK on this experience, I wonder whether I might have avoided the landing of this great and awful bird. Had I made the decision to look the other way, once I suspected its character, might I have circumvented the attack of this dismal mood?

Perhaps we are like birdwatchers, peering into the distance, up into trees, behind bushes, staring through our binoculars for incoming avian varieties. When we see what looks to be an interesting specimen, we zero in on it in the same way that the mind will treat a thought. We can guess by its plumage, its flight pattern, its song, what genus it is. There is a moment, as with a well-studied birdwatcher, when we are able to identify the incoming thought. At the same time we understand its habits; we've made a careful scrutiny of the various species. If the bird is of a dark character, if we have witnessed it pushing the other birds' young out of the nest, stealing food from fledglings, harassing and mobbing, we are naturally put on alert. "Incoming!" our spirit sounds the alarm, "Incoming mean-ass-bird thought." At which point we might best look around for a place to hide.

Unfortunately, as with my pterodactyl, these thoughts are vaguely seductive. There is a sick sort of curiosity, the slightest fascination with the incoming horror, which allows the monstrous beast time to make purchase. We engage in a flirtation of sorts with the darkness. Perhaps this is what is referred to in the line in the Lord's Prayer, "lead us not into temptation." Help us to lower our binoculars and run for cover. Better yet, help us to find another bird on which to focus, a lovely, bright, colorful thing with a perfectly beautiful song.

However skillful we become at early identification and swift-footed dodging, I'm afraid that at some point in our lives most of us will find ourselves flattened by a pterodactyl. At which point, there is nothing for it but to ask for help. These old birds are heavy lifting.

13

The Great Leveler

When parents complain about their children, it typically has something to do with the fact that their child acts as if the world revolves around them. I suspect this attitude comes naturally to a child raised in a healthy home. The love of the parents is rightly focused on the child's needs. Freshly arrived from the divine world, the child may justifiably sense that the growth and care of their spirit is of grand importance to the heavens, as important as the whole of human evolution.

As the child begins to approach adulthood, this sense of being the center of the universe can and often does increase, inspiring feelings that are confused and unhealthy. This is when the "isms" move in, when the grown child finds herself wrestling with narcissism, and materialism, finds himself battling egotism and hedonism.

This is when a young man surmises that he must have been sent into the world for a specific calling, when a young woman wonders whether she might have been carefully chosen to be God's gift to the world. This idea isn't necessarily a negative. The conviction that one might have been born to save the world can drive some people to do very good things.

I fell in love with the stage as a teenager, and it wasn't too long before I began to wonder whether I was meant to be God's gift to the theater. Egotism aside, I honestly suspected the theater was my calling, that I had somehow answered a summons from the heights of the heavens and come down expressly to fulfill this role.

After many years of frustration, I can see that the theater was God's gift to me. It taught me most of my most important lessons. I have learned more from failure than I ever could have from success, and am very grateful for this learning. But, I am now on the other side of this learning, looking back, and not in the middle of the "isms," where it is very difficult to see and hear clearly, the isms are just so very large and loud.

When I see someone in their 20s or 30s suffering from the "isms," I don't get as concerned for their souls as I used to. I try not to fret over them and to fear that they will never learn a single lesson during their time on earth, because I believe that the Great Leveler is always watching, and has a plan up his sleeve. Let me explain…

I see our souls as great, gorgeous, empty fields. When

we arrive here these fields are pristine, gently sloped, full of wild flowers and soft grasses. But, there are very few who can keep these fields in their natural state of purity. At some point most of us will allow the isms to have their way, or, to follow the field metaphor, will allow the pigs to move in. Now, I love pigs, they are fine, noble creatures, but their strong rooting noses are amazingly destructive to a leveled field. Pigs are relentless, and can take a field as smooth as a pond and make it look more like a storm-tossed sea in just days.

The good farmer who is watching out for his fields is keenly aware of any destruction, and notes the condition of the land, the soil. But he waits and watches.

At some point we will awaken to all of our splendid flowers and delicate grasses lying uprooted in our fields and will shudder to realize how hostile our soil has become to new growth.

The farmer still waits. He has the ability to send in the tractor, level the land, and yet he waits for us to ask for his help. If we ask, the leveling could be painful, it could take time, depending on the state of the field, it could be frightening, but afterwards, the field will return to its smooth, naked state. It is at this juncture, when our fields stand naked in the sun, before the flowers and grasses have begun to return, when we are given a choice. We may choose to let the field rest and recover its splendor, or allow the pigs back in.

Whatever the choice, the farmer will be watching, always watching, and waiting for an opportunity to send the tractor back in and level his beloved land.

Bill Wilson, founder of Alcoholics Anonymous, suggests it is at this point, just after the leveling, and before the field grows back, that one can begin the process of turning one's life around. You don't have to suffer from alcoholism to understand the wisdom of this. Bill suggests that we take this moment to be honest with ourselves—in fact he says that we must be honest with ourselves, with one other person and with God. I would say this is true when we are wrestling with any of the isms. If we don't face ourselves, the pigs will make their way right back into our fields.

I was once invited to help a friend at the birth of a litter of piglets. The mama, Pancetta, was beginning to make nesting movements, tearing up grass with her teeth and creating a bed for the arrival of her babies. Piglets at birth are between eight to ten inches from snout to tail, and Pancetta delivered eleven of these tiny packages in the space of a little over an hour. After a sow delivers her young, she allows them to nurse for a bit, then stands up for a nice stretch, looks around for a bit of water and food, and collapses from exhaustion. This is a dangerous moment for the piglets. If they are under foot, as they often are, they can be crushed by the great weight as the tumbling mama crashes to the ground. My friend and I were aware of this danger and attempted to herd the little ones into a corner of the shed while Pancetta turned around, looking for a soft place to land. When one of the little piglets attempted to dash underneath her, I plunged to my knees and reached both hands around him. I was completely caught off guard when this piglet, not even an hour old, began to drag me along the floor of the shed. Forty minutes old, and well under a foot from nostril to tail, he had the power to upend me. I did manage to keep him from being crushed, thank God, but was quite impressed by this display of barreling strength.

The isms are born with the same sort of strength. Their potential to grow into three hundred pound, bone-crushing animals is clear from their arrival. If we allow the little things access to our fields, they will undoubtedly end up rooting up all of our beautiful flowers.

Our only hope, I'm afraid, is to appeal to the farmer. "Please, we might say, please help me, I let the pigs in, and they have grown to thirty times their original size. They are destroying your beautiful field. Help, please!"

Help will come, you can be sure of that. The farmer is always watching.

Pieces of the Puzzle

14

Necessary Souls

When I was in first grade, my teacher read the class a story. She then handed out little pieces of paper and read three questions, which we were to answer with multiple-choice selections. We marked the little box next to the correct answer, and she collected the papers, looked them over, and announced that the class could go out to the playground. All but me, she added. She wanted me to focus on one of the questions and see if I could give her the correct answer. She was a nice person, and I didn't mind this sentence too terribly. I returned to my seat and attempted to puzzle out the answer, but the longer I thought about it, the more I was convinced that my answer had been the right one. These textbook tests are so often ambiguously written. Finally, I walked up to my teacher's desk and explained that I could not see how the answer could be anything other than the one I had given, and I explained why I felt as I did. She listened to me (she really was a kind woman) and thought for a moment. "You're right," she said, "the others answered the question incorrectly." She didn't apologize for her own part in the story. Perhaps she felt the confession was apology enough.

When my classmates returned, I waited for the teacher to explain what had happened, or at least to revisit the question and attempt to look at the answer from another perspective, but she avoided the subject entirely. I remember little of my early years, but this day in first grade stands out in sharp contrast to the rest of my dreamy days in primary school.

It seemed to say so much to me. I sensed that the teacher felt that she was in an awkward position. If she had returned to the subject, admitted to being wrong herself, set things straight with the rest of my class-mates, her power would have been slightly shaken, and she might have lost a bit of authoritative ground.

I am not sure whether this was the original seed that was to grow into such a sprawling disdain for authority, but the plant, a hearty vine now, has crept into every corner of my world. I have no patience with authority figures, no tolerance for dogma, no time for pedantry. Emerson would be proud, not because I so willingly ac-cept his axiom of self-reliance, but that I resonate with this philosophy so profoundly that I take him as a true friend, and go my own way. "*Trust thyself*," he encourages, "*every heart vibrates to that iron string.*"

I met a woman once who told me that she was taking a summer course on intercessional prayer.

"What is that?" I asked.

"Prayers offered for divine intercession," she explained. "Most are prayed for those suffering in the hospital, who may not have anyone else to pray for them."

"How lovely." I said, "but you say, you are being taught how to do this?"

"Yes, it's a six-week intensive. At the end, I should be able to walk into any hospital and pray for anyone who wishes it."

How very odd, I thought. How long has prayer been offered as a six-week elective?

I walked away from this meeting in baffled wonder at the human need to complicate.

But couldn't she do this now? I thought. Is there a lesson plan for such a thing, a particular prayer curriculum? Does this mean that my own prayers for intercession have been denied because I didn't receive a degree?

Plblbpblp!!! Nonsense, I thought.

But, what a kind person this woman must be. I have to wonder, though, why would one seek mediation for the intimate connection between one's soul and one's God. It would be like asking a conductor to orchestrate one's breathing, taking a class on proper laughing techniques.

Perhaps this is why I prefer my teachers dead and

in print. It is almost impossible for them to stand on false authority. At any moment I can pitch them in the wastebasket.

I spoke to a minister once and told him that after years of struggling with despair, I had, through the practice of prayer and trust, managed to attain a level of contentment that was for me quite lovely.

"That's grace," he responded. After further discussion I understood him to mean that this feeling was all gift and had nothing to do with my daily efforts, and that this offering might appear or disappear at God's will, or whim.

But, if there is such a thing as free will, I thought, why should I not conclude that this grace was a result of my meeting God halfway? And furthermore, why should I trust another to pinpoint the mysterious, ever-shifting threshold where I end and God begins?

"*The faith that stands on authority is not faith,*" warns my good friend Emerson. "*When good is near you, when you have life in yourself, it is not by any known or accustomed way; you shall not discern the foot-prints of any other... The way, the thought, the good, shall be wholly strange and new.*"

Such a grand friend to have!

But I confess, even my good Ralph Waldo has said some things that have made me recoil. The beauty is, I know that he would applaud such a reaction. I can see him. He would leap to his feet, throw his arms above his head, clap outrageously, and whoop and encourage:

"*Whoso would be a man must be a nonconformist,*" he would holler. "*Insist on yourself.*"

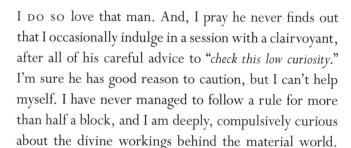

I DO SO love that man. And, I pray he never finds out that I occasionally indulge in a session with a clairvoyant, after all of his careful advice to "*check this low curiosity*." I'm sure he has good reason to caution, but I can't help myself. I have never managed to follow a rule for more than half a block, and I am deeply, compulsively curious about the divine workings behind the material world. Any hint that I might extract from whatever source available seems worth the transgression.

Here is a little story to illustrate.

When I was twenty-three and living in New York City, I met and fell in love with my husband, Matt. Several months later, he moved back to his home state of Tennessee, and I assumed that this was the end of our relationship. Some time after Matt left the city I had what I would call a light date with a young man. We were walking around the West Village, and on a lark we decided to enter the door of a palm reader. At that time there was a handful of these psychics on every block and we randomly chose the door nearest us. The woman inside was quite ordinary, in street clothes, (no turbans or faux gypsy garb). She took my hand, studied it for half a moment, lifted her head and looked at me.

"You are in love with a man who has moved away," she said.

I shuffled in my seat, aware of the young man next to me.

The woman continued to look at me. I took a breath and returned her gaze.

"Wait for him," she said. "He will come back to you."

Back out on the street my date turned to me. "Is that true?" he asked. "Are you in love with someone who has moved away?"

"Yes," I admitted, a tad embarrassed. "Yes, it's true."

My husband did of course return to me and we married nine months later.

It seems that when the Divine has a message to deliver, any voice will do.

Of course there are other means of divine communication. There have been times in my life when silence was more pregnant with message than any number of words spoken.

Several years ago on my morning walk in the woods I had such an experience. I had been gathering essays on spiritual themes for many years, and I was having a tough time placing these writings.

I must assume that I am not the first to find sitting and scribbling down one's ideas a lonely process. Please don't feel sorry for me, I am well-befriended. But along with the attempt to gather my thoughts on faith came the fear that no one would ever benefit from them.

When my nose was to the ground following some divine thread, I was quite content, but the moment I raised my head to wonder where this was all leading, I would feel the chill winds of doubt. After many years of writing and failing to find readers, my courage started to lag, and the voice that would have had me believe that my thoughts would never reach a single soul was the only one that I could hear.

One day this voice was particularly cruel and piercing, convincing me that I might as well put down the pen that minute and admit defeat—there simply wasn't a place for me in the world conversation.

I was walking along my familiar path in the woods, one that I walk daily, when this hopeless thinking grew so heavy that I felt as if I were carrying a crushing physical burden. I could barely lift my feet and feared I was about to crumble into a heap of despair. I stopped, steadied myself, and said out loud, "I just can't do this alone anymore."

Not three seconds passed before I felt, but did not see, a presence arrive at my side, a being who carried a feeling so loving, so deeply compassionate that I was overwhelmed with the sense of sudden and profound empathy. I knew that this someone was even more intensely sad for me than I was for myself, one hundred times as sad. This willingness to share so heavily in the weight of my sorrow caused me to be instantly, keenly embarrassed. I felt the need to apologize to this heavenly presence, and the next words out of my mouth were "Oh dear, I'm so sorry to make you so sad. Please forgive me."

I'm not sure how long I was in the company of this presence, perhaps only the space of three minutes, but this experience had left me weightless with relief.

Two years later, a friend recommended a clairvoyant to me. It was near my birthday and I arranged a phone session with her. Before I called, I decided not to ask anything specific (I was still frustrated by the obstacles to finding an audience for my writing) but to simply ask, "Why is it that I'm here?"

She spoke, uninterrupted, for an hour, while I listened.

"Once," she said, "several years ago, you were very unhappy, you were alone, and you cried out for help."

I held my breath and listened.

"And," she continued, "you said out loud, 'I cannot do this alone.' Do you remember?"

"Yes," I answered.

"Now, this is where you may have a difficult time believing me," she continued. "In fact, I am having a difficult time believing what I am about to say. Someone came to you, a presence."

"Yes," I repeated.

"This being was Saint Teresa. Saint Teresa of Avila. Do you know anything about her?"

I admitted that I did not. I was not raised in the Catholic Church and do not know my saints. Neither did the clairvoyant, she admitted. She couldn't tell me much about Saint Teresa, but she continued.

"Apparently she comes to those who are in great despair. She is a being of great empathy, and is drawn to those in anguish. She brings absolute compassion."

I could not disbelieve her.

Of course, I cannot know the truth of who it was that visited me that day. The identification of the saint is minor next to the confirmation of divine attendance, and the message that was conveyed. Principally, that we are not alone, we never have been alone, we never will be alone. Our sorrows, goals, frustrations, fears, even our joys are held... by whom? I'm not sure that it matters. By another, by one other, by more, by more than just ourselves.

15

Awakening

When I was in my twenties, I worked in a little theater company in Manhattan's Bowery. This was during the eighties when the Bowery was home to a large number of men known as Bowery Bums, alcoholics who lived in the dozens of flop houses in the lower East Side.

I would pass a handful of these men every day on my way into and out of the theater. Depending on the time of day, I was either acknowledged by a word or two thrown in my direction or I drew no attention at all. By the end of the day these men were typically too high to focus, and I would walk by them, seemingly invisible.

I was young and quite self-involved at the time. I don't remember stopping and really trying to imagine what sort of life might have brought them to this place. Subsequent decades have enlightened me as to how very difficult life can be, and how much men like these need our full-hearted compassion.

One evening, when I was leaving the theater at about eleven o'clock, several of these men stood on the corner of Bowery and Bond Street. They looked to be well into the late-night stages of blind-drunk. As I drew a little nearer, one of the men suddenly careened off the curb and began to fall into the street. At the same time a taxi was approaching at a wild pace, and the two were about to collide. I was a half a block away and knew that I could be of no physical help, so I screamed.

"NO!!!" I yelled at the top of my voice. At which point, instead of falling into the road, the man fell back on his rear end on the curb. Plop. Disaster averted.

I stood with my hands over my mouth, shocked. The men did not turn around to see who had screamed. They were so far gone that they probably never even heard me, let alone notice that their friend had just missed being run over.

I stood panting for some time, recovering.

The truth is, I was undergoing a sudden and cataclysmic awakening. When this man began to fall into the street, he transformed completely from a person to whom I paid little heed to someone who was as precious to me as anyone has ever been in my life. He was my brother, sister, husband, mother, and if anything had happened to him as horrible as I thought was about to happen, I would have borne the scar of not having helped him for the rest of my life. I would have cursed that half a block between us until I died.

This incident had illumined the place where this man and I were connected, where true kinship resides.

In that moment I uncovered a very clear truth: no matter what we appear to be doing with our earthly lives, no matter how important, or unimportant we appear to society, we are all exactly the same size.

If seen from the heavens, from a place of pure love, we all carry precisely the same weight, all take up exactly the same soul-space.

Looking from the flatlands of our earthly view, our short history on the planet, we might think that Mahatma Gandhi, for instance, was a bigger soul than this man, suffering from alcoholism on the streets of the Bowery. But, of course, this is a complete falsehood.

WE ARE PIECES of a huge puzzle, each of us. Every one of us is the same size, with the same portion of spirit allotted to us. And, like pieces of a puzzle, we fit in our places perfectly, with our small indentations and protrusions, our stalactites and stalagmites, our tiny portion of varied color fitting precisely in our little slots within the puzzle's pattern. We are just the right shape for our lives, allowing us to fit in with the people who surround us, within our life span, our present age, geography, history, current events. No one bigger than the next, no one more dear.

If you have ever put together a jigsaw puzzle you know that if one piece is missing, just one, the entire puzzle, all the work you have expended putting it together, seems worthless. And, if you have ever come near the end of a puzzle and realized that there was a piece missing, you understand the willingness to crawl around your living room floor in order to retrieve that errant piece, to enlist the entire household to comb through every area of the home in order to locate that one delinquent piece. The search could go on for days, the piece must be found.

This is how, I am convinced, we are viewed and valued from the heights of the nonphysical world. There is no shape, no pattern, no fit like you, no one precisely like you.

This is a truth that keeps me engaged in the act of living. I can look back across the landscape of my life and see several dramatic instances where, had I not acted, spoken, or stayed up at night with a friend who was suffering, a precious piece of the puzzle would have been lost, and the whole lacking.

I can also see less dramatic times, thousands of them, where I said something, did something for someone that set that person on a slightly different trajectory, almost always without my knowing it.

On the receiving end, I have been lifted out of despair, set back upon my path, and directed in hundreds of life-saving ways, by the smallest encounters. Often when finally thanking someone for saying that one key something that turned me around, I am met with a blank stare.

"I said what?" they ask, "And that helped?"

Most often the help that we offer one another is off-hand, an organic reaction. It is hardly ever planned, organized beforehand. Sometimes it can arrive in a scene played before us, as with the man who was almost killed by the taxi, without the characters involved being aware that they are offering enlightenment. Looking back at the averted collision on the Bowery, I can see that even lives that many would consider wasted can, by their presence on earth, be an instrument of significant awakening for another. Some very subtle meetings reverberate for many years after they occur, often with far-reaching resonance.

Several years ago a friend invited me to join him for an opening of a Broadway play. We both have some connection to the theater and the invitation was accompanied by various warnings and apologies concerning the less-than-flattering advanced reviews picked up along the theatrical grapevine.

There is the danger, when one scrutinizes an art form too closely, of dissecting the life out of it, as a child-scientist would a frog. At the end of a bad night at the theatre, the frog lies in pieces about the stage as you limply apply palm to palm in polite sympathy. After a good night the frog has transformed itself into a prince and you have leapt to your feet to applaud the miracle. This particular production was rumored to be a science project.

On the way to the theatre that night, my friend and I shared our own wrestlings with this child-scientist, and resolved to attempt to quiet the critical mind and remain open to the possibility of magic.

We were joined at the theatre by my friend's acquaintance, a theatrical agent whose proximity to the business of theatre allowed him just enough inside information for some hair-raising gossip. The theatrical nobility is as closely watched as the royalty of England, and the subsequent tattle can be as shocking as anything printed in a London rag. I was mistakenly introduced to this man as having rubbed elbows with some theatrical royals with whom he had reportedly locked elbows, and after hearing a choice selection of gory reminiscences, I spent the time before the play trying to convince him that I really didn't "know" these people, that it was probably best that we try and preserve the last residue of their dignity by changing the subject. The subject was finally kicked aside but its replacement was much the same: who was of importance in the world of the theater and how low they were willing to stoop. Somewhere near the end of this awkward conversation we took our seats, my friend to my right and his acquaintance on the other side of him, the seat to my left remaining unoccupied. The lights dimmed, I took a deep breath, and attempted to open my mind to the first act of the play.

It was intermission when I again found myself in the company of the Person of Disturbing Inside Information. My friend had disappeared and left the two of us outside the theatre, looking out over a sea of New

Yorkers, dressed in their uniform black. I once heard New York aptly described as a city in mourning. My companion was tall and scanned our fellow mourners as I struggled to find some safe subject on which to engage him. I eventually commented on the fact that one doesn't see people "dressing" for the theater anymore, not even for openings. Scrutinizing the crowd, he replied, "Well, there's no one of any real importance here, anyway." At this moment I looked to my left and noticed a little character shuffling through the crowd. As small as a nine-year-old, a man of middle years, dressed in a tiny brown suit, pushed his way along the sidewalk. His movements were labored owing, it appeared, to some crippling illness. His size, suit color and carriage made him as striking as a wildebeest moving among a flock of penguins. I watched as the penguins parted slightly and without notice to allow him passage. Fascinated, I continued to watch the little man's awkward journey until he was lost from my sight.

The lights soon flashed and I joined my friend to discuss the first act of the play. We concurred, unfortunately, that we had entirely failed in our attempts to bury our scalpels and that it was far too late to piece the frog back together. While we were making our furtive comments on the production's entrails, I became aware of some slight commotion in the seat on the other side of mine, the seat that had been empty during the first act. I turned to investigate and discovered my little character in the brown suit carefully lowering himself onto its cushion. This took considerable effort on his part, which allowed me time for some undetected examination. The face was hidden to me, so very tiny and hunched over was his form. A slight odor arose from him as if he were unable, perhaps due to his physical difficulty, to bathe himself daily. Once nestled into his seat, his ear barely reached my shoulder and his chin hovered somewhere near his chest. Overcoming my natural timidity with strangers, I decided to speak. I mentioned how nice it was that someone was able to use the empty seat, and wondered how he had managed it. Because of my towering relation to him, my words were directed to the top of the man's head. His physical limitations were such that he had first to twist his head slightly sideways before he could lift his face to meet my own. I carefully braced myself, expecting to feel some shock of sympathy, but was unprepared for what I saw. The man's face was one of exquisite beauty. The smile, which was offered immediately and without any prompting on my part, was divinely lovely as he explained that he worked for the theater and was given this seat for the second act as a gift. As I basked in the warmth of that celestial face, I thought how innocent the man must be to view his seat at this production as a gift, how enviably innocent. I said again how happy I was that the seat was occupied and settled in for the second act.

At this point I remember secretly thanking the heavens for putting this man next to me and not, for example, next to the Person of Disturbing Inside Information. I was feeling protective, as if someone might be tempted to judge this man on any attribute other than the light that shone from his face, as if the sum total of his oddities and beauties would add up to anything less than the most important person in the theatre that evening. Because you see, after this brief encounter, I was thoroughly convinced that this was indeed who he was.

The second act began and I continued my battle with the inner-scientist, the struggle made twice as ludicrous by the presence of the man to my left, who was himself the picture of respectful attention.

After a rousing victory on the part of the scientist, I suffered through the obligatory standing ovation that occurs after most Broadway plays, not knowing whether to join the enthusiasts and feel hypocritical, or remain seated and feel like a damper but retain my scientific dignity. I believe I chose a combination of the two, proving myself a sort of damp hypocrite. The applause and my embarrassment having subsided, the audience began to move slowly toward the exit and I followed, leaving my new friend behind me. As one of the last to leave, I turned at the door to see if he was still there. Indeed he was. He stood across the empty theater, in the same spot where I had left him, as if he were waiting for me to acknowledge my departure. When it became clear that this was precisely what I was doing, he once again graced me with his beatific smile. I remember responding with my own grossly inadequate one before I left the theatre. I have never heard of or seen the man since.

One might be tempted to ask, is that all? My answer would be yes; yes and decidedly no. Yes, that is all that occurred that evening. But no, this is not all, because the events themselves don't begin to explain why I have thought of this evening hundreds of times over the last several years or why I am moved to write about it now. The closest I have come to an explanation is that I dearly wish to live in a world where this man might one day be revealed to have been the most important person in the theatre; a world where a night at the theatre might always be viewed as a gift, simply by virtue of the theatre's potential for transcendence, by its power to lift us out of our seats in the delight of this great mystery; a world where the truth might break through illusion in the time that it takes to look a man in the eyes, and change a life forever. And somewhere within me is the strong suspicion that, if looked at more carefully, this is the very world in which we do live.

16

The Good Father

M y brother called the other day, "So who are you
praying to these days?"

"Oh, something between the Native American Great
Spirit and a big warm-hearted Daddy," I said, knowing
that this answer was as temporary as the day.

"But what are you calling him?"

"Today?" I asked.

"Of course," he responded.

"Well, this morning." I explained, "I referred to him
as "Dear Heart." A line of Emerson's states: *the heart in
thee is the heart of all*." How nice, I thought when I read it.
Perhaps that's what I will call God tomorrow.

"Do you ever pray to a mother figure?" my brother
asked.

I confess that this isn't the first image to grace my prayers. Not that I think this Great Spirit with whom I converse daily doesn't have a feminine side. The difficulty is, when I was a child I believed that God the Father and Mother Earth were an old married couple, and I can't shake the picture.

My brother, on the other hand, has spoken of engaging the feminine face of god. I remember one period in particular when the Virgin Mary featured heavily in his prayers.

I am reminded of a friend's son who was overheard in church singing, "Holy, holy, holy, Lord god is ninety."

Whatever keeps your boat afloat, I say.

"And what sort of prayers are you praying?" my brother continued. "Are you still saying the Lord's Prayer?"

"This morning?"

"Of course."

"This morning I did not visit that particular prayer," I said without compunction, "In fact, I dashed past all worldly concerns, and dove right into praying for myself." I went on to confess that I had lately been in need of a bit of heavenly direction, and what with the time constraints on my morning, I'd wallowed in a session of beggary.

I explained that I had made use of the rather simple prayer, "Please guide me this day." And then added, "I would like to be useful, therefore I am counting on you to tell me what you would like me to do, and make it very clear, please. You know I am no clairvoyant."

"But," my brother interrupted, "what if you are asked

to do something that you really don't want to do? something that goes against the grain? Aren't you leaving yourself open to difficult things?" My brother thinks of everything.

"Well, I always add a line or two to parry any such thorny direction," I answered. "For instance, I might add a line to this effect: Now, you understand me, right? You are aware of my strengths and weaknesses. Some say you created me, for goodness sakes, and therefore I presume that you will keep in mind my parameters of usefulness, most importantly, my fears and repulsions. I am not, I warn, like Don Quixote, prepared to '*march into hell for a heavenly cause.*' In short, I expect that you will fit the deed to the scaredy-pants instrument."

This notion appealed to my brother. I knew it would, as he relishes even less than I do any departure from the comfort zone.

Of course I would love to be braver. I look forward to a day when I am able to offer myself up for anything: cold phone calls, long board meetings, and tight elevator rides (I am a timid claustrophobic who suffers from instant meeting-room narcolepsy). But today, I can only be so willing. Or perhaps I should say, I can be very willing, but as with a prescription drug, I expect the list of side effects to be thoroughly weighed and considered.

But, this willingness, I believe, is an important first step, and I do try and offer this daily.

As a child of God the Father and Mother Earth, it seems to me that they've been married long enough, have raised enough children over the years to have gathered some smarts. I don't think they would intentionally ask me to do something that would land me in a mental institution, like, say, trap me in an elevator after a long meeting. I have to trust this, but then, I am about in the third grade in a twelve-year school of trust.

Some day I hope to be terribly bold and make daily, joyful leaps toward my destiny, but I'm just not there yet. In fact, one day I'd like to be like Romeo, who, having had a dark premonition of his future, yet raced toward it with all of the bravado of a two year old. He tore across the square and into the Church to marry his bride, shouting to the heavens: *"He that hath the steerage of my course, direct my sail!"*

I could be like that some day, sure. But for now, please, no elevators.

MY PRAYERS HAVE gone through numerous small shifts and leaping changes over the years.

Recently I realized that as much as I claim to believe in an all-loving father figure of a God, a good parent who wants the best for his children, who guides and nurtures us, I wasn't addressing this being during my daily communications with the heavens.

My prayers, I discovered, more often sounded like appeals from a slave to its master. "Please, please, please, give, grant, take away, don't punish, I don't deserve, I do deserve. If I do this today can I have tomorrow off? No? Then what can I have?"

A master might be tempted to give something to a slave simply to shut her up—perhaps I was unconsciously banking on this. A good parent knows just the right amount of freedom to allow, can see that it would be unwise to hand a thirteen-year-old the keys to the car. A good parent knows that the best time to give is not when the child believes he deserves the gift, but when the child can handle its weight. A good parent can see the possibility of our soul, and is willing to wait for its unfolding. A good parent has the patience of eternity. Damn.

I wrote a play eighteen years ago. It was a humorous look at one of my favorite subjects, the question of an afterlife. I call it an end of life comedy. As with all of my plays, I prayed that the piece would fall into the right hands and be given a good life. The owner of those hands I was imagining as a sort of director-producer prince with shining theater connections. I performed all of the necessary duties: took a good year to complete the first draft, fussed with it for another year, mounted a reading with good actors with substantial reputations, invited the right people. There was a little flurry of interest, and then nothing, silence. At the same time, I must confess, there was a good deal of master-slave beggary. "Please, please, doesn't it deserve... don't I deserve... I've done everything right, haven't I? Please don't punish me. Give me, give me, give me, give me."

A year went by, two years, then five years... but no prince came forward to fall in love with my play, to kiss it awake, bring it to life.

And so I picked up the pen to write nonfiction instead, shoved the play back into the far reaches of my closet where I'd stashed my other manuscripts, and attempted to believe that I had never written them, or more optimistically, that the plays were simply the soil from which my nonfiction might grow—so much loam, so to speak, but nothing in themselves. Then one day, God knows why, and I do believe that God does know exactly why, I fell back in love with the theater. I was watching a friend's play, a good play, very funny, performed by a fine group of actors, "Uh oh," I thought, "I think that little door, the one that I shut all those years ago, I believe that thing just popped open."

When I got home I dusted off the play that I had written all those years earlier and asked a friend whether he might consider helping me put together a production, whether he would direct the piece, if we could find a place to mount it. I had never worked with him before, I just had a hunch that he would be very good. I spoke to another friend who suggested I mount the piece in her big cathedral space of a barn, where we had worked before in partnership on various cultural events to raise money for Haiti. I liked the idea and decided to make the play a gift to my neighborhood. I wanted to work with people I cared about, in an atmosphere of harmony, and present the play to a community that I had come to love.

Lots of friends came forward to help me, friends I had never realized could perform the tasks that they were offering to perform. A dear friend, one whom I knew as an actor and a poet, happened to be a stellar stage manager, another whom I had only seen perform serious roles, ended up being a wonderful comic actor. My director turned out to be the perfect partner for me. Everyone seemed to wish to be involved, and they gathered, some from the neighborhood, and others from across the country, even though the project, performed in a private barn, would never "further anyone's career."

It was a tremendous amount of work, involving half a year of planning, but oddly enough (and if you have ever been a part of a large collaborative effort you will understand why I say oddly) all of the people I wanted to work with were available at the same time, and everything fell easily into place.

At some point in the final week of rehearsals a good friend came into the barn, which we had been working furiously to turn into a theater, and said. "Why doesn't everyone do this? If we were all busy putting on plays for one another, we would have no time for all of those empty pursuits, like making money for money's sake, shopping for more stuff, waging war." I could see her point. I began to see our play as a kind of peace project.

Eventually the play was performed on three evenings for an invited audience. The first night was full and joyous, the second was more full and even more joyous, and the third night was sheer joy, with people hanging from the rafters. I had never before seen one of my plays so beautifully realized. The production felt as if a magical spell had been put on it by a good theater fairy. It was a gift from beginning to end, and even in our challenging moments, which are always part of putting on a show, a dozen or so unique souls remained in supportive harmony with one another. Hallelujah.

As I look back at my years of frustration around my plays and my long hiatus from the theater, the timing of my heart-opening, and the events that followed from it, seem so finely worked out by the heavens, that I suspect the project would have been a colossal failure had I attempted it even seconds before. I can see that before this moment I wasn't prepared to be a proper steward of this, or any of my plays. I hadn't the confidence. I needed years and years of quiet nonfiction work to pound and mold myself, to cut away any unnecessary insecurities. And I sense that something similar was true for everyone involved. We all had to have reached a particular moment in our lives before this happy production could have been achieved.

I think I'm going to drop the slave routine, and start addressing the good father like a proper child. "Help me please, to realize what's best for me," I might ask, "in the time that it is best for me to realize it."

"Oh, and please... help me to share in your good patience."

17

Lasting Dreams

I have always had an easy faith in the continuation of the soul after death. This conviction doesn't appear to demand any of the typical maintenance that other beliefs of mine require. Life eternal exists as a reality for me without effort and for this bit of grace I am eternally grateful.

I could cite some early influences that might explain such a comfortable surety. My grandmother, for instance, had a near-death experience in her early years, and her story may have biased me at a young age, but I don't remember learning of this until I was older. I will share her tale with you now because it's one I would wish to hear myself.

The time was somewhere during the mid-nineteen-thirties, and my grandmother was somewhere in her late twenties. She was in labor with her third child and was taken to a Catholic Hospital In Louisville, Kentucky. There were complications with the delivery and the choice had to be made as to which of the two (mother or child) would be given the best chance of surviving. It was a policy of this hospital to make the greatest effort to save the child. My grandfather, fearing for his wife's life, called an ambulance to carry her to another hospital, and while she was in route she died, at least in the clinical sense. Floating out of and above her body, she looked down to find her husband weeping over her remains, and drifted farther away. The rest of the story is a bit vague but at some point during her journey she came across her mother, who had died ten years earlier. She was holding a baby girl, and said to my grandmother, "I'll take care of this one." Whether my grandmother spoke to a being of light or encountered any of the other phenomena which are so often reported of such experiences, I cannot say, but she was given to understand that she must return to her body and young family, and that all would be well with the child left in the spirit world. She did return to reassure my grandfather that all would be well with her, but that the child, a girl, was not to live—a fact with which she was strangely at peace. As often results from such experiences, my grandmother was much changed, with a fresh trust in the workings of the universe, and the life eternal.

I must assume that this confidence was passed on to her family, as all of us have a comfortable approach toward the great crossing. I hope this surety will continue to touch future generations, as I hold it as one of the sweetest of earthly gifts.

If I imply that I have never doubted, I am not being entirely truthful, for I have plunged into the very depths of doubt, but only once, and only for a few hours. I was eighteen at the time and taking a Shakespeare class from a gifted professor, a man whom his students respectfully addressed as Dr. Adamany. There were moments in Dr. Adamany's class when I imagine the Great Bard himself would have leapt to his feet in surprise at his own genius. It was in this class where I first learned to recognize the divinity behind a chosen combination of words, that deep ocean of truth on which floats all transcendent writing.

I believe it was King Lear we were studying at the time, or was it Hamlet? I do know that it was one of those plays that deals an awful lot with mortality. Whatever the play, we had been focusing that day on death, and specifically the fear that most often attends the idea. After class I came up to Dr. Adamany and said, "But not everyone fears death, do they? I have never feared death." To this he replied, "You are young and so far from your end. When you get to be my age," (he was somewhere in his late fifties), "you will have grown to fear death."

"Fair enough," I responded, and went back to my apartment to brood. "So, all of this confidence," I ruminated, "this comfort in the continuation of my spirit, will slowly drip away as I age?" I gasped, "How dreadful!"

That night I tucked into bed in a dreary mood. I had experienced very little death in my eighteen years, and most often it had occurred to people who were much older than I, and who seemed to me to have lived a full life. I did know of one boy my age who had committed suicide when he was fourteen. I will call him Lenny. Lenny had been a neighbor of mine up until we were both around eight, when my family moved away from the neighborhood. After this I never saw him again. Six years later my mother informed me that he had taken his life.

On my night of creeping doubt, I fell into bed, exhausted from worrying over the grim notion of life transient and drifted off to sleep. Sometime in the wee hours I had a very vivid dream. I have noted that my dreams come in four specific variations: the profound, the prophetic, the downright lunatic and the disincarnate visitation. The latter are the most rare. If you've ever had a visitation dream you will understand what I am attempting to describe. Often they are quite mundane. I will be simply sitting, having a cozy chat with someone, when I realize that that someone has, for some time, been supposed dead. On this particular night I was sitting and talking with Lenny. He was a good deal older than when last I'd seem him, in fact he appeared to be my age, as if we had grown older together. And, even though I hadn't laid eyes on him for ten years, he was so very, very Lenny-ish. Again, if you have ever had such a dream you will be able to relate to this portrayal. These visitors appear more themselves than ever they appeared in life, as if you were being visited by their purest, individual essence. I can't remember what Lenny and I were speaking about, but whatever the conversation, I suddenly interrupted and exclaimed, "But Lenny, here we are sitting and talking with each other, and you're supposed to be dead!" And he answered, "Oh Margaret, you know better than that." And, it was immediately after the delivery of this very simple statement that I popped awake. Another aspect of these visitations is the sudden snapping shut of the dream door and the subsequent wide-eyed alertness. I sat up, reflected, concluded that I did know better, and never revisited the doubt again.

I have always been fascinated by the subject of the hereafter. I consume near-death stories like candy and have studied scores of mystics on the subject, one favorite being Emanuel Swedenborg. Swedenborg was a household word around the mid-eighteen hundreds in America, in part due to the interest of Emerson and his fellow Transcendentalists. A century earlier, Swedenborg had been a respected Swedish scientist, who in mid-life began to experience visions of the spiritual world. He spent the second half of his life writing reams of often baffling narratives about his journeys into this mysterious realm, but on the subject of the life to come he could be painstakingly specific. The soul, he claimed, traveled first to the spiritual world, and then, according to the person's "affections" (a term which could be taken to mean love or passion or even interest), either moved toward, or away from God. He does employ the terms "Heaven" and "Hell," but these are to be understood as an infinite number of states of being, related to the overriding loves of the human being. He goes on to explain that we will be drawn to people and land-scapes that reflect our inner selves (these selves being so entirely transparent that hypocrisy is an impossibility). The levels of "Hell" therefore are freely chosen for their correspondence to our loves. Those in Swedenborg's Hell would not describe the place as such, but simply the place where the soul feels most at home. Sweden-borg roundly denied the horror of eternal damnation, claiming rather an eternity of opportunities to change direction, both ascendant and descendent, making all of life, on this side and the eternal other, a hesitant sailor's tack toward enlightenment.

One of Swedenborg's notions that I find particularly delightful is the concept of aging in the world to come. When a soul crosses over at a young age, he writes, she will grow older and into her prime, but if she lives to the ripe old age of ninety, she will age in reverse, grow-ing younger, back into her zenith. Our true spirit bodies (which he claimed were megatons more real and alive than our earthly ones) appear and behave as the ideal thirty-five-year-old. I love this idea, and have often heard it reflected in stories of dreams and visions of those pre-sumed to be dead. In fact I had one such dream myself.

I had a friend who was somewhere in her sixties when she died, about twenty years ago. Up until her death, she had worked as a cook for my mother, who had hired her when I was a teenager. She was an African Ameri-can woman, five feet tall and nearly as round, with the bright, open face of a ten-year-old. Her name was Allie and she was a favorite among all who came to our house.

Those who knew her always chose to enter through the kitchen, in the hopes of an indulgent Allie visit, before announcing themselves to the rest of the inhabitants. She was a fierce champion of equality and commanded a respectful position among the members of my family and all who visited our home.

Allie and I were very close, and she often introduced me to newcomers as her "Baby."

Allie took the feline approach to death and brushed against it nine times before it took her. She had been in and out of the hospital with complications, due mostly to asthma and the devastation of the drugs prescribed for it, before she gave up the fight.

In the late eighties, shortly before she died, I went home for a visit. Entering, as always, through the kitchen to have a nice chat with Allie, I found her much the same. She said that she had been well but mentioned that she had been hearing voices.

"Whose voices?" I asked.

"Dead people's voices," she answered.

"For instance?"

"My brother, Mother, friends."

"And, what do they say?" I prodded.

"Nothing much. Sometimes they just call my name."

I took careful count of the number of close calls she had weathered. Just about eight, I figured. Two months later those voices called her home.

Several years ago, perhaps ten years after Allie's death, my friend Patricia was visiting me in Pennsylvania for the weekend. Many years before, when I was in college,

I had brought her home to Louisville. She had naturally taken an immediate shine to Allie, and would occasionally ask me about her, although she never saw her again. One night during Patricia's visit I had a dream about Allie. It had all of the trappings of a visitation dream. Allie and I were having a comfortable chat when she pulled a Polaroid snapshot from her pocket and began waving it in front of me. "Look, " she said enthusiastically, "this is what I look like now!" I studied the photo, which revealed an Allie that I had never witnessed on earth. She was in the perfect prime of life, as healthy as a young doe, and finely proportioned, looking as if she might have just had a light skip up the side of a mountain. 'You look wonderful!" I exclaimed, and then shot out of my dream, keenly awake. I smiled, grateful for this glimpse of an old friend, and drifted happily back to sleep.

The next morning Patricia came down from her room and, after a bit of coffee, remembered a dream she had had that night. "It was about that wonderful woman who used to work for your mother, her cook. What was her name?"

"Allie," I replied.

"Yes, Allie," she went on. "This was Allie, alright, only she was about thirty-five and at least a third of her weight."

"Allie was busy last night," I answered, and went on to share my dream.

I OFTEN ASK friends to search through their own histories for such dreams. My friend Sarah had a visitation dream of her father, which was long, luscious and full of spiritual wonders. If she hadn't needed it so much at the time, I could throttle her for not immediately taking pen to paper and recording every marvelous detail for me. Sarah was visiting her mother at the family farm on lake Michigan the summer she had the dream. Her father, a gentle English professor, universally adored by the family, had died several months earlier on Christmas day. Since that time, her mother had been quite lost and the mood around the house was empty and mournful. After several weeks of pervasive sorrow Sarah was given her dream.

She was walking along the pebbly shore of the lake near her family home when, at a slight distance, a door appeared, a single door, suspended above the beach. The door opened and just inside stood her father. Directly on course with such dreams, he was radiantly healthy, and looked to be somewhere in his hearty prime (an age Sarah could barely remember his ever being). He gestured for Sarah to come to him, but when she neared, he warned her that she was only to step just inside, she wasn't to venture beyond this point and mustn't stay too long. After their initial joyful greeting, Sarah began to ask him questions of his life on the other side of the door. Unlike other dreams she might have had of her father, she was very much aware that she was speaking with his departed soul.

"What do you do here?" she asked, "how do you spend your time?"

"It's difficult to explain," he answered. "Time here is not as you sense it on your side of the door. You might, if you dearly loved something, such as a poem, for instance, spend a month with that poem." (Sarah's father had been a great lover of words.) He continued, "Almost, you could say, spend a month inside the poem."

He gave her to understand that those passionate interests that you uncover in your life on earth are further pursued in the coming world; the discovery of what you truly love in this life is of vital importance to the continuing soul.

She asked him other questions, which he attempted to answer, but he warned that no earthly explanation could begin to describe life on his side of the door because (and he was to repeat this several times), "Your world is just a suggestion of this world. This," he stressed, "is the real world."

During this conversation, Sarah made sneaky little attempts to trick her father into letting her stay, trying to inch past him and move further into his world, she had missed him very much and it was all so inviting. Each such attempt was gently parried by her father. "No," he would say, "it isn't your time."

She woke suddenly from the dream, much relieved of her heavy mourning, still feeling the comforting presence of her father.

The atmosphere of the house that day soon began to eat away at her comfort, so she decided to leave it and take a walk. Perhaps, she began to doubt, this dream had simply been the contrived fantasy of a mind in grief, and not a real encounter with her father.

As she stepped out of the sorrowful house for her walk, Sarah asked for some sign of encouragement to believe in the dream, the truth of which she had been so convinced during the experience. She asked specifically that the sign be in the form of a large bird. Birds had always symbolized the spirit for her. The walk was long and meditative, but brought nothing unusual, no avian wonders, and she turned back toward her mother's house with diminishing faith. When she entered the front door her mother called to her from where she sat at the kitchen window, transfixed by something she was studying outside. "Come and look," she urged. "He's been sitting there since you left the house." Sarah approached the window, and just outside, on a near tree limb, sat a very large owl. Entirely uninhibited, the great bird stared with fixed gaze at the two women inside. The sight of this nocturnal creature in the middle of the day was a great rarity (typically fleeting and mostly hidden, they are secretive, light-shy animals), but the steady, answering gaze, at such close proximity, was almost unearthly.

The owl wasn't to move from the window that whole day, finally taking off at dusk to fly low over the area where her father's ashes lay scattered. Sarah and her mother learned later from a neighboring birdwatcher that no such owl had been spotted in those parts for years.

IN MY COLLECTION of such dreams, there doesn't seem to be any sort of time limit for the return visit of a departed soul. My aunt Mina, who was widowed in her early twenties, had her first and only visitation dream of her deceased husband, my mother's brother (whom everyone called Possum), over forty years after his death. Mina was well into her mid-sixties at the time of the dream, and the two old lovers sat together looking through pictures of Mina's life since Possum had left the world. Mina had since married twice, had two children and several grandchildren. Content now, with a large and loving family, Mina was able to show Possum how her life had played out since his departure and show him all of the love she had gathered. Possum seemed genuinely pleased for her and assured her that he too had found happiness. Toward the end of the dream, Mina called my grandmother (Possum's mother) to tell her that her son had not in fact died all those years ago in a car accident, but that he was still alive, more alive than ever. My grandmother (who had left the world fifteen years earlier) replied, "But of course dear, I've known that for years."

I love such stories. I hope, by the end of my life, to have collected such a comfortable pile of them that I can tuck in amid them like a puppy with its litter, and drift dreamily into the everlasting.

18

Desert Island Thinking

I caught myself postponing a prayer recently because I thought it premature. I had been asked to give a talk at a rather large gathering, and I tend to be rather shy of public speaking. I needed help from the Heavens. "Oh, but that won't concern me for a good three months," I thought to myself, "nope, I won't begin to pray that for another... oh, nine weeks or so, when I'm about two and a half weeks out." I stopped short of adding the prayer date to my datebook.

This moment gave me pause.

For those who have had near-death experiences, waking epiphanies and prophetic dreams and who try to share them with others, the most challenging concept to put into words is the difference in the nature of time in the world of spirit from time as we know it in our waking state.

Earthly time is awkward enough for us to grasp—note the disparity between the length of a day for a seven-year-old and someone who is fifty-seven—but imagine trying to explain the complete absence of any construct of time. Impossible.

Consider a native man who has lived all of his life on a small island in the deep ocean. The island is just the tiniest tip of the great mountain beneath (imagine Kilimanjaro) and the island dweller is familiar with only one billionth of its surface.

Trying to explain that this moment in earthly time could not exist without the foundation of all time (past, present, future, eternal) would be like describing to that man that his existence there on the desert island could not be possible without the foundation of landmass beneath him, and the eons of time in its creation.

All of us live on that island.

I had a dream many years ago that I was in a large room, a restaurant of sorts, with three walls of floor-to-ceiling windows. I stood looking around, trying to figure out where I was. The windows appeared to look out at sky, and nothing else. "I must be in a spaceship," I thought to myself, "but a restaurant in a spaceship?" I had only begun to wonder at this, when suddenly the floor moved violently beneath my feet. "An earthquake?" I thought. "An earthquake in a restaurant? In a spaceship?" I continued to try and wrap my head around this puzzle when one of the waiters walked to a door on the side of the room. He opened the door to reveal a set of descending stairs. He looked down them, and then turned back to those of us in the restaurant and said, "There is no way out."

No one panicked. We absorbed the information in silence, gently turning to look at our fellow prisoners. Five seconds later I woke up.

I knew that the dream held some sort of disturbing significance and made sure to tell Matt about it the next morning, feeling as if the strange thing should have a witness. One day later the country suffered the attacks of 9/11.

It wasn't until a few days after the attack that I remembered the dream. The only place I had ever visited in the World Trade Center was its rooftop restaurant, Windows on the World. The restaurant had floor-to-ceiling windows on three sides and a view of open sky.

I have since read somewhere that if you feel disturbed and don't know why, the wisest thing to do is to pray. If you have a troubling dream, feel a sudden, unfounded anxiety, groundless despair, stop for a moment and offer up a prayer. "Bless us all," you might say, "God help this world."

The reason for this feeling, dream, intuition might be that something as yet unformed is threatening to occur. Perhaps it won't happen for twenty, fifty years, maybe not until after your time on earth, but the moment to pray is now, when the intuition arises. Maybe your tiny prayer will help avert a possible, future disaster, or help those who will be caught in the calamity. Perhaps the earth needs just one more ounce of positive thought to add to the foundation of positivity that supports us, a necessary addition to the landmass of prayer that holds up the delicate balance of harmony in this world.

I used to think of a prayer as being a bit like a single balloon. My morning prayers were offered one at a time, and released like rubbery round shapes full of helium into the heavens, red for this friend, blue for that, green for our good Mother Earth. I would watch them rise, assured of their skyward direction and hopeful of their timely arrival in the heavens.

Since the moment I caught myself in delaying a prayer, my notions of the timing of communication with the divine have shifted. I have had inklings of future events, premonitions, déjà vu, prophetic dreams throughout my time on Earth, and the timing has varied from something that will occur the next day to twenty years in the future. Why would this not be true of a prayer as well?

We are still on the small island, and our understanding of the world behind the physical is so very constricted. Einstein would agree. "*The most beautiful thing we can experience is the mysterious,*" the great scientist said, "*(He) who can no longer pause to wonder or stand rapt in awe, is as good as dead.*"

I hereby promise never to reschedule a communication with the divine. If the thought arises today for me to pray for someone, or some issue, I will assume it is because the timing for this prayer is perfect, the conditions ideal, no matter how many seconds, or centuries, it might take to resonate.

In fact, I think it might be time to throw out many of my frozen ideas.

SEVERAL MONTHS AGO, I spent a week at a retreat center, a sort of summer camp for adults, with a focus on mind, body and spirit. Every day all types of classes and presentations were offered to about 130 guests. I met a full array of different varieties of people, from the young to the ancient. And, I discovered that like a crack speed-dater, I was very sharp at categorizing each one within the first seven seconds of introduction.

"Oh she's the type that prefers to focus on the body rather than the mind," I would say to myself. "He's one who would dismiss any of the contemplative offerings altogether."

To try and help me to break this ridiculous habit, the heavens kept contradicting me.

"Gosh, I'm surprised to see that woman on a meditation hike," I would say to myself in mind-stretching puzzlement. "Wait a minute, that guy is taking introduction to watercolor? I never would have guessed. Hold on, those two came to the casual sing-along?"

By the end of the week I had had all of my tidy summations about the entire population of guests blown to little bits.

It became clear that this process was also happening to other campers. We shared communal tables for meals, and the question would come up about which programs people had enjoyed the most. One very grounded woman with a high-powered, government job in DC confessed to having broken down in tears during a class called "Sound Healing," a program that she would have dismissed as "woo woo" the day before. "I was surprised at how much it did for me," she sheepishly admitted. "It opened up an old wound that I thought I had dealt with, but it had obviously just been buried."

Oh, and just to let you know how un-evolved I am, I had dismissed the program altogether because I over-heard that its teacher, near the end of the one class, sug-gested that the participants (quote) "marry themselves." "Oh, no, no, no I won't be going to that class." I said, "I would find that keenly embarrassing."

Why do we do this to ourselves?

I was travelling with two good friends, one of whom had bravely attended the final class of "Sound Healing" and had much the same reaction as the high powered woman from DC—she really loved it. Dang!

Why hadn't I tried it? Why do I limit myself so?

THERE WAS A young woman whom we befriended mid-week, in her late thirties, and apparently the prankster of her family. This family had shared a highly unappealing doll that had been used as a practical joke for decades. It would present itself in the most unlikely places, once in the face cradle of a massage table while this woman's un-suspecting sister lay down to have her body rubbed. Not long ago, this woman confessed, the doll had shown up at her grandmother's funeral. It had occurred to her that it might be hugely funny if, at the cemetery, while the family was throwing in little handfuls of dirt on the casket, she were to whip out the doll and throw it in along with the earth. She knew that the grandmother would have been the first to double over in hysterics, with the rest of the family following suit. The stunt succeeded, giving the family a much appreciated yuck fest.

Later in the week of summer camp, I learned that this young woman was member of a rather strict orthodox Christian sect, and had spent much of her time in her room with her bible.

"But these two facets of her personality are too contentious to fathom," I thought, as the door to my mind groaned on its rusty old hinges.

Like someone wearing pink pants and a bright orange sweater, she clashed!

But then she isn't finished. None of us is. We will wear all sorts of discordant ideas, try on all manner of philosophical combinations before we find just the right harmony for our souls.

I HAVE COME to understand that, more than anything else, it is my frozen notions, my rigidities, that keep me from growing. These are what retard my movement toward enlightenment.

While thinking about writing this piece the word

"disabuse" kept popping into my mind. Disabuse… disabuse… I have found that my muse (angel, writing spirit, spiritual scribbling cohort) will often toss a word into my head while I am forming my thoughts around a piece of writing. These words are almost always ones that I have never used, the meaning of which I am not at all sure.

"Disabuse…" I wondered, "why is that word coming up?" I had to look it up. Disabuse: to free from deception or error; to persuade that something is untrue.

My brother told me about an interview he had read with the Dalai Lama, where the interviewer had asked, "What if you get to the other side of death and discover that your theory of reincarnation was all wrong? What if you discover that the truth is that we do not return and return to the earth, and therefore you could not be the reincarnation of the original Dalai Lama?"

"Then I would let go of the idea and accept the truth" was the Dalai Lama's simple answer.

Clearly he is very comfortable with being proved wrong.

This has me thinking that I might have discovered my next daily prayer. Dear God, please disabuse me of my calcified notions of how you work in this world. Surprise me, please.

Please don't ever let me think that I am finished.

19

Story Time

I sat in the Philadelphia airport wondering if I should wait out the promised delay, or just go home. Various phone calls had been made: to my sister and brother, who I was to visit for the weekend, my husband, who offered to come and fetch me if I wanted to come home. It was up to me, they all told me; I just needed to let them know what I wanted to do. After staring off in space envying the travelers who whizzed around, seeming so sure of where they were heading, I dug around in my wallet and extracted a penny: heads I should put up with the delay, tails I should go home.

Toss. Tails. "Tails, I should go home... Hm."

"Maybe I should toss it again?" I reasoned... Toss. Tails. "Tails, I should go home..."

"I'll just toss it one more time. Toss. Tails. "Tails, I should go home…" "Hm," I mused.

Half an hour later my sister called. "What have you decided?"

"I still don't have a clue." I answered, limply waving away my mind fog.

Though I'm typically a snappy decision maker, the power to choose a course of action had abandoned me.

"You don't sound so good," my sister added.

"No," I agreed.

"I think you should go home," she concluded.

"You think so? Probably." I said, continuing to sit heavily in my metal seat.

I hung up and had a similar conversation with my brother.

"I think you should go home," he advised.

"I imagine you're right," I answered. I got up and proceeded to noodle around for another half hour in the terminal, absently tacking my way down to ground transportation.

Several hours later, from the comfort of my home, I discovered that the flight I had deserted had ultimately been cancelled.

This would make that penny toss right, I suppose, but this is not a tale of penny augury.

The story, and lesson is: when you are sad, stay at home and be sad. Don't skip out the door, hoping to bounce around the sad. Sad is something that must be plowed through at the point of sadness, otherwise it will be heaped up and stored somewhere, only to be dealt with at some less convenient date, in some lonely airport, surrounded by preoccupied strangers.

Two days before my attack of airport catatonia, Matt and I had helped our beloved Labrador Tater to cross the bridge into the next world. And, although she was ancient and I had been praying for months for her gentle release—"Swing low sweet chariot"—one is never completely prepared for these things, and her absence weighed like a heap of dense heaviness on my heart. It scrambled my thoughts and temporarily stripped me of my will to direct myself.

Most of my readers will understand this. I have met only a handful of people who cannot imagine that one would mourn the passing of a pet as profoundly as the loss of a human. In some cases this grieving will be more intense than what we feel for our human friends, but then we often spend more time with our animal friends and are dependent on their presence in ways that we would never allow ourselves to depend on people. It wouldn't be fair to burden our human friends with so much daily neediness.

In considering how I might begin to lift the weight of this sadness, I concluded that more than anything I needed stories. Initially I searched for stories from people who felt as I did, stories of mourning. "I couldn't lift my head from the pillow for a month after I lost my dog,"—those sorts of stories. The ones that make you feel perfectly justified staring off into space for hours, crying at television commercials, playing the same sad song again and again. Stories that allow you to stop what you are doing and feel, for however long you must feel. The writer E.B. White was still writing about his dachshund Fred twenty years after his passing.

This sort of story-medicine helped, and after a nice indulgent draught, I figured I would need hopeful stories, those, for instance, of departed pets visiting their owners in dreams, joining them in near-death experiences, appearing in visions. I needed reassurance that this was not a final parting, just a pause in Tater's and my relationship.

Having been graced with a few such experiences, I know their power to lift.

Most often my visitations have occurred in dreams or glimpses out of the corner of my eye. I have also heard the occasional familiar bark, felt the dull thump of a long-departed cat jump onto my bed. I would like to share a few tales to add to the story-medicine chest, in case you ever find yourself struggling through the dim mind-mist of pet grief.

When our dog Happy, who left the world several years ago, first came for a dream visit, the scene was the little sunroom where she used to sleep. I sat on the couch and in she walked from the living room, head low, full-body wag, the corners of her mouth rising slightly toward her ears. It was the position she would always assume when showing her deepest affection. "Happy's here!" I gleefully yelped, and snapped awake. Joyous.

The second time Happy visited by dream, the scene was the same: in she walked, head down, body wagging, only this time I was able to give her a long, satisfying hug. My husband had a similar dream of Happy within a few months of my own. In she walked, healthy, wagging. He snapped awake, grateful.

Just before Tater crossed over, Happy made an appearance that I caught out of the corner of my eye. I was on my morning walk and there she suddenly was, trotting along her familiar path in the woods. I turned to face her, and my vision evaporated. I presume she came to show her friend Tater to her new home.

Once, after my husband and I had been married for many years, I had a dream that a glorious, shiny-coated male collie sat outside our door. He seemed rather larger than the collies that I had known, and his coloring was a deep brown and black. When I woke I asked Matt to describe his old family dog, Flash. "He was a collie, but larger than most, with black markings," Matt said.

We were away from home and our dogs at the time. Perhaps Flash felt we needed protection.

Two days after Tater died, I was walking my young Lab Cotton on our familiar trail through the woods. A couple that I occasionally see there stopped and asked whether I had two dogs with me.

"No," I answered, "why?"

"Because," the man told me, "I thought I saw another darker lab with you, sort of a shadow of a lab."

"How lovely." I answered, and explained.

Love, reciprocal love, is an open door. I cannot believe that death has the strength to shut it. Death is a feather-weight pushing at the gates of a fortress, impossible.

"Too late," I say to death, "too late. Love has blown the hinges off."

Confirmation

20

Showing Up

During World War II, an American Sunday School teacher who was serving in the military in the Pacific captured a Japanese soldier. In marching the man back to camp, the American discovered that his prisoner spoke English.

The Japanese soldier, on hearing that his captor was a Christian, told him that he used to be a practicing Christian as well.

The American soldier responded, "and you no longer are?"

A look of surprise came over the face of the Japanese soldier. "But, how could I be a soldier and still remain a Christian?"

I am drawn to the place where faith and ethics meet.

The weather can be quite unpredictable at this juncture. The fog rolls in regularly and causes us to lose our bearings.

When George W. Bush was in the White House, I was particularly troubled by the fact that one who would claim to be a Christian would relax the laws on torture. That Christianity and the justification for torture could be linked within the same person seemed monstrous. That these two ideas could exist anywhere near one another was impossible. Therefore one of them, I concluded, either Christianity or torture, must be a lie. I wish I could say it had been torture.

As one who occasionally attempts to write about this uneven territory, I know it is a very delicate procedure to explore the ground of faith and ethics without seeming to cast shame on my fellow travelers. By holding up an impossible model of spiritual perfection, we cause those who walk beside us to run away from our words, leaving us to trudge along alone, stumbling through the deep-rutted landscape of our own hypocrisy.

I'm sure I have never met a perfect Christian, Buddhist, Muslim. The fact is we are all duplicitous. We all live somewhere between our finest, openhearted intentions and our weakest, stingy-hearted, knee-jerk reactions. And, although it is important to be discriminating, to recognize the duplicitous in others, none of us can claim to be immaculate.

WHEN I WAS a teenager and attending a progressive Episcopal church, our confirmation teacher, a wonderful, bold man, suggested that we walk into the Sunday service and ask the parishioners whether they would answer a question. Our class dutifully filed into the service and waited as this man interrupted the proceedings to pose his question: "Those who believe in God," he said, "those who truly believe, raise your hands." To my surprise, only one third of the congregation did so.

I have thought about this moment often over the years. My first reaction as a teenager was, "Well then, what on earth are the other two thirds, the ones who aren't so sure of God, doing here?"

Now, this had more to do with my desire to sleep in on Sunday mornings than any sort of spiritual righteousness. Why, I wondered, would these people have dragged themselves out of bed on one of the precious days when they might have slept in, in order to be fed an hour's worth of medicine that they could not swallow? After all, I, who did believe, wanted nothing more than to doze through the ordeal.

My attitude about the congregation's answer has more recently grown into respect. "How very open-minded of these people," I have concluded.

We aren't born believing. Faith is like a very slow-growing tree, first the seed needs to take root and then the spindly little seedling requires years and years of sunlight, water, pruning. Just when we think our faith has established itself, something will come along, some great crushing storm, and test it to the limits.

Although I would have been among the number that raised their hands that morning, and have never wavered in my belief in a power of love and wisdom greater than myself, I cannot always see my way clear to doing the right thing, thinking the right thoughts. I assume this is why I show up at life every morning. To learn a little more about God. To try and clear away the fog of my hypocrisy. "Just keep showing up," I tell myself, "the weather is bound to clear."

I love the newly discovered text of the ancient Gospel of Thomas. Thomas seemed to have taken from Jesus's teaching one resounding message: "*Therefore I say that if one is unified one is filled with light, but if one is divided one will be filled with darkness.*" And "*Make the two into one.*" He encourages, "*When you make the two into one, you will be called the sons of men. When you say, 'Move, mountain' it will move.*"

One doesn't see mountains scooting around the landscape very often these days.

I now understand those who claim to be Christian, Muslim, Buddhist, or, as I would describe myself, "Everythingist"—that is, one who is in love with all of the great faiths. I now see us all as followers. We are following the precepts of our various faiths. We are being led. We are dragging ourselves out of our sleep-drenched beds every morning in order to learn a little more about God. The fog will clear someday, the weather brighten. Trust this, and keep on showing up.

I HAVE A friend who tells me that she is an atheist. When I ask her what that term means to her, she tells me that she "doesn't believe in a God," but she does believe in a great web that connects everyone, every being, every life form on earth, and that anything that occurs to one part of this web, affects the whole.

"Some might employ this affecting principle to describe God," I respond.

In fact, the word "God" might be interpreted in six and a half billion unique ways.

My suspicion about those who avoid the word "God" is that they have heard the term hurled around by too many careless people, or had it repeatedly slung in their faces over the years. Some, I also suspect, have observed the word being so furiously avoided by those they admire that they step around it themselves, like a large pile of dog refuse.

The language of the divine has been a sticky wicket since the concept of that larger "Something Other" first came up. It has served to invite and repulse for centuries, sometimes with the most god-awful, stake-burning consequences.

To understand why this might be, I sometimes imagine a disco ball. We're all familiar with these revolving orbs comprised of tiny, flat mirrors, designed to reflect sharp points of slow-moving light. These reflections, depending on the terrain over which they travel, will appear sometimes distant and sometimes near. They will dance frantically over a rugged landscape and sail smoothly along the gentle, yet the intensity of each individual pinprick of light is the same.

Now, imagine if one of these tiny pinpricks asked another one to describe the cause of its existence. One might point to the tiny mirror that appears to be responsible for his reflection. Another might point to the small spill of light at his own feet, or that of his neighbor. Several might reach up and point to the fraction of the bright orb above them that they are able to see. Others might be aware of the entire round shiny ball. Some might reason that behind such a magnificent sphere, there must exist a great source of light, one that they cannot see.

"How," one pinprick might ask of another, "do you know that there is a grand source of light behind all of this?" He waves his hands around.

"Because," the other pinprick answers, raising her arms out slightly, palms up, "I glow."

The first pinprick looks at his friend, observing her small portion of radiance as it travels over the neighboring surface. He looks down at his own tiny pool, its pale shining. "But," he returns, "Couldn't you glow, because of that?" He points at the large, revolving ball.

"But that is only a great, round mirror," she answers.

"Is that how you see it?" returns the first, as he peers up at the revolving ball.

"Yes," she continues, "The sphere is simply designed to reflect."

"Hm," he ponders.

"Therefore I presume," continues the lady pinprick, "that there must be something other, some original source that ignites the orb and causes us to twinkle "

"But couldn't that be called life, called existence?" he asks.

"It could be called whatever you wish. I do not wish for words to stand in the way of our understanding one another."

"Then shall we call it spirit?" he offers.

"What a fine idea, yes, that will do precisely... for now."

The point is, they cannot see, cannot prove, can only imagine and describe through symbol and metaphor what they sense to be the cause of their own fraction of light.

The language of the spiritual will morph and sing, then sputter and shift, only to regroup and trumpet itself by popular demand. Words and phrases will go in and out of favor. Lately, the language of the divine seems to be going through a rather vague phase. Among my friends the word "Universe" replaces the word "God," as if the word "God" were not ambiguous enough. But then, words are so fragile and the miracle so huge, the weight is often crushing.

This spirit, this grand wellspring of existence, without which we would all be as lifeless as those deflated plastic lawn ornaments that lie in the December yards of American suburbia, is notoriously tricky to define.

The trickiness could have something to do with the

seemingly preposterous history of life on earth. The chances of the evolution of life on earth moving along its hair-thin course, from the Big Bang (a huge madcap miracle in itself) to this morning's eye-opening, bed-exiting phenomenon are fabulously remote, like an elephant's journey across the ocean, balanced on a cobweb. Our existence on earth is a baffling miracle, we will never come up with language to capture such colossal creativity.

There are some people, writers, many of them, who can speak of the spirit behind all of life without embarrassing either themselves or their audience. This is a rare gift. The truth of their convictions so beautifully supports their language that they can press even the hottest of buttons, "Satan," for instance, "sinful," without offence. Perhaps this is because their language is second to their intuitive understanding—the language serves the ideas, not the other way around.

I have for many years loved the writers of the mid-eighteen hundreds, and lean heavily toward their language. The Scottish writer George MacDonald, with his lovely expression the "Father of Lights," is a particular favorite. But I do understand that many may find his language overly sentimental, and so I hesitate to recommend him to any but a few, because—and here's where the wicket gets sticky—one can get stuck on a word and never reach the point.

Perhaps our stumbling language is a necessary obstacle. Like the disco ball and the individual pinpricks, it protects us by its very clumsiness from the annihilating

power of direct light. In fact, if the orb were t[...]
out of the way, we would not be able to retain our i[...]
viduality in the presence of the great original source and
there would be no self left to describe it; all would be
awash in light.

Doesn't sound half bad, does it?

As one pinprick to another, I suggest we celebrate the
creativity of our awkward attempts at naming, and embrace each other's metaphors.

o move
di-

21

Light-Bearers

I have been following closely the story of Malala, the Pakistani girl, and now Nobel Peace Prize recipient, who kept an online diary of her life under a two-year Taliban rule over the valley where she lived, during which all girls were forbidden to attend school. Malala carried through with her blog from the age of eleven amid constant death threats. She told the press that she did not fear dying in the cause of enlightening people around the world about life under Taliban rule, and for the rights of Pakistani girls to have access to education. In the fall of 2012, as she was on her way home from school, several members of the Taliban boarded Malala's school bus, asked for her to be identified, and shot and critically injured her. When she was brought to the local hospital, hundreds of people came to donate blood. The country of Pakistan prayed and bore witness to this atrocity. And, because the world is so closely connected these days through the international press, many millions around the world shared in this witness, including me. Sunlight, as the old adage goes, is the best antiseptic.

One can look at this story from many angles: "Such ignorance! Such violence!" "Such, such bravery on the part of the girl!" "How could they? The monsters!"

It's tempting to focus our empathy on the victim: "God bless this girl! Send her healing!" "Send her light!!" and to toss the perpetrators, the monsters, into hell.

But everything inside of me tells me that light, like prayer, if properly handled, must be sent without division, without partisan ties. Light, God's light, cannot be targeted in the way that the US military tells us that it targets the enemy. This is not a drone attack, but a prayer. And, prayer, if it is to have any effect, must affect all involved, which in the case of this story comprises the entire country of Pakistan. That includes, yes, I must admit, the ones who are gleefully taking responsibility for the attack.

Malala's story reminds me of our country's witness of the attacks of 9/11. I remember watching that day unfold with a stunned, confused feeling, paralyzed by the horror of the attacks, but unsure where to direct my thinking. In the ensuing weeks friends told me that they had been crying constantly, mourning for the victims and their families. I wished that I could join them in a good cathartic cry, but something was blocking the way. I felt almost dead inside.

It wasn't until two weeks after the attacks that something happened to awaken me. I stood in a parking lot of a vet's office and observed a woman attempting to get her dog out of her car. He was a big yellow lab, and given my love for canines, and the fact that I was living with two of the same color and breed, I stopped to watch her. In what seemed an unwarranted anticipation of bad behavior, the woman clicked the leash on the dog's collar and then took the end of the leash and angrily whipped the dog in the face several times before she let him step out of the car. I stood watching the scene in horror, unable to say or do a thing, as if my feet were nailed to the ground, my mouth plastered shut. The woman then passed with her dog into the vet's door and left me standing in the parking lot, tears streaming down my face.

The scene opened a flood of emotion: for the dog, for all helpless animals, for the victims of 9/11, the families that were left to mourn, the firefighters lost, their families. But it did not stop there. It couldn't. The flood seemed to take everything with it. It loosened and lifted up everyone involved: the perpetrators of the attacks, the families of these angry young men, the boiling rage around the world, the ignorant, the violent, the cruel, the unthinking, this woman. I knew I had to do something with all of that chaos, all of the people who were carried along on the waters of that flood. I vowed to pray for everyone involved in the hatred that led to the atrocity of 9/11, and for those affected by the cruel action, a number that seems to encompass the entire population of the world. I also promised to pray for the woman who was so cruel to her dog (and for the dog himself, of course), but I knew that the light I sent must go to both of them. I couldn't target him without affecting her. Prayer, like light, cannot be divided.

I have thought of this woman at least a thousand times since that moment, and whenever I do, I pray for light to rain down on her. At this point I have sent this woman half a sun's worth of light.

One cannot go wrong with light.

Apparently there were prayer vigils going on all around the country of Pakistan for months after Malala's wounding. I pray my own small effort aided in penetrating the darkness surrounding her story just a hair deeper than if I did not exist. If I keep up the shining on my end, I hope after so many years to fill buckets full of light, enough to share liberally among all Pakistanis, and other world citizens, enough to shower the innocent and the monstrous, enough to light up every corner of the world.

FOR MUCH OF my life I have made regular visits to a certain remote island in the Atlantic Ocean for the privilege, among many, of observing the night sky in relative, unpolluted darkness. On perfectly moonless nights it is difficult to see between the stars, so densely packed they are, with the Milky Way appearing like a bright sidewalk across the heavens.

On my most recent visit, during the semi-darkness of a mid-moon-phase, I lay on my back watching the half star-pocked sky as the occasional cloud motored across my view. I watched for some time, hoping for a meteor, some wild, bright ride across the heavens (a frequent gift of this place), when suddenly my perspective entirely upended. Instead of looking up at the dark, star-graced sky, I was in the heavens, looking down upon the earth at night, peering down through the slippery clouds onto a great expanse of open, black sea where the lights of the stars had become sailing ships, their lamps bravely clinging to their swinging masts. The ships appeared sometimes densely, sometimes sparsely scattered across the vast, dark water-scape, their tiny lights announcing their existence.

Just as the brighter stars help to form the constellations, so the steady beacons of the greater ships appeared to gather groups of floating communities about them, the accompanying, dimmer mast lamps giving more or less shape to the design. The ships with the most intense concentration of light, the mighty ones, those we might name Castor and Pollex, Regulus, Sirius, appeared to pull the smaller, neighboring ships into purposeful society.

When I am home under the anemic, light-saturated skies of my home on the Eastern seaboard of the United States (the most densely lit sky-scape in the world), only the brilliance of the greatest stars can reach me. I wonder at the great ones' consistency, their ever-full, bearing light, their ability to hold massive quantities of radiance without doubtful sputter. Their steady shining comforts me and reminds me of the great multitude of brother and sister stars, those whose light is not able to reach me, but who exist nonetheless, those fainter friends whose slight glimmering I can see when I take the time to visit my quiet, dark island.

That night, as I lay imagining this dark expanse of water-dense earth beneath me, cheered by the presence of these bold clinging lamps, I could see that each light shone as brightly as it might. Some might blink and fade, some might shine with steady intensity, but all were from the same source, the same light, the property of light being light.

I could also see that some lights, some of the weaker, flickering ones, floated adrift in shadowy isolation. I felt a certain compassion for them. The vast number of tiny ships seemed to be taken care of by their family of sibling ships, which formed small societies. I pitied the ones adrift by themselves, those who, I imagined, hadn't seen the light of another ship for weeks, months, years even, those travelling on the night's ocean without a beacon, a heartwarming glimpse of another on the horizon on this weak-mooned night. I imagined how comforting it might be for them to catch sight of another ship's lamp in the distance, to find that they weren't alone after all. How, I questioned, how could one be convinced of the presence of a sea full of lights, when one had been so long adrift, without the comforting vision of a light-bearing companion, on this unbroken night sea?

I can't imagine who I might have been without the encouragement of certain sources of light along my own night's journey. Many have been writers. Ralph Waldo Emerson, for instance, with his steady surety, intensity of light so powerful that my own disheveled doubts have been known to shrink away in its presence.

"*Oh my brothers, God exists,*" he proclaims without a flicker of reservation. "*There is a soul at the center of nature, and over the will of every man... Place yourself in the middle of the stream of power and wisdom which animates all whom it floats, and you are without effort impelled to truth, to right, and a perfect contentment.*"

But, this is a rare gift, this combination of grand light and giant intellect, like those huge stars whose magnitude is visible even under the opaque skies of the over-developed world. Thankfully there have been other, smaller lights, living souls who held their gentle shining high enough for me to see along my own obscured horizon. Often when I seemed to be drifting aimlessly in sweltering stillness for days, weeks, months without helpful breeze, they have arrived with the reassurance of their cheering lamp.

When I was a child one such beacon shone from a dear friend of the family, an artist, raising two children on an artist's wages. She was gentle and humble and, no matter what sort of darkness was raging at the time, she was always ready to point to the brighter reasons for existence, the possible wisdom behind this paradoxical, often difficult life. I can't bring to mind anything specific that she said to convince me of this luminosity behind all existence, just a tendency, a leaning toward its truth. In retrospect, I imagine she might have wrestled with many of the same doubts that I have met in my adult life, and yet she was able to hold her light steadily enough for a child to see that it was possible to live a life of pervading light.

This radiance doesn't have to be a grand display of faith and sacrifice, but can be something quite small and practical. There is a woman who has worked in my neighborhood vegetable stand for at least the past twenty-five years. She greets everyone who enters with a generous, embracing warmth. Her light is made of kindness, her gift is a certain consistency of positive mood.

It has occurred to me lately that this is enough to give the world in payment for all it has given us, this light-bearing. We don't need to produce pyrotechnics, practice award-winning generosity. We just need to lift up our own particular light. We need to try and hold it steadily enough so that its spill might be a comfort to another—sometimes literally, for just one other. This is enough, this small light-bearing for the one other.

"A little lamp can fill the whole house," the Haitian saying goes.

22

Sunshine

It had been a year and a half since my yellow Labrador Tater departed our home for the next world. Tater had left us with Cotton, another yellow Lab, who was only five at the time, and accustomed to being part of a pack. After a month or so of mourning, I began to pray for another dog to join our family of animals. I wanted the animal to find me, rather than the other way around.

I knew myself well enough, and my instant, head-over-heals infatuation with any creature that spends five minutes on my native soil, (or as some might call it, my yard), to know that I could never return an animal if I discovered that it didn't fit in our family group. I was presently suffering the fall-out from my refusal to find another home for a cat who was launching daily attacks on the other two felines in the house. My only hope was to hand over responsibility to someone with a more elevated perspective.

I began to pray for a dog to come to us. Preferably in some sort of obvious way, arriving on the doorstep, for instance, with a sign around its neck with our names on it. I hoped for a dog that would fit perfectly with Cotton, with me, with Matt, and one that my cats wouldn't taunt too mercilessly. I prayed that the new dog would be calm, like Tater, and that she—yes, I wanted a girl—would be deep and thoughtful. Doesn't hurt to ask. I prayed that she would be unmistakably right for us.

I know of a man whose old cat passed through the great door after something like twenty years, and he swore that he would never get another cat because the death had so devastated him that it nearly caused him to follow his old friend through the door himself. He stuck to his resolve to remain cat-less, refusing to allow the thought of a feline to enter his head for years, when one day he was standing in a New York City subway station, waiting for the train, and a kitten fell out of the ceiling tiles above him and landed on his head. Of course, you know the end of this story; they are enjoying a lovely, long life together. This would go to show that you don't have to be praying for something in order for it to come your way. The heavens know our needs. But I say, why not engage them? Perhaps we can be more a part of creation, and not just a recipient. Perhaps we can begin to work together, the heavens and us.

I spent many a morning walk in my local park begging for a new dog, but doubting whether I was being heard. I would repeat my lengthy preferences in temperament, and add a new one to the list almost daily. Most important to me is the Labrador's tendency to stay within sight of its owners. The breed has many annoying qualities, I must admit: they need an enormous amount of exercise to be good housemates, and would chew a house down to its foundation, if allowed. But, they rarely leave you weeping in the woods. Because I take a walk every morning in my local park with my dogs off leash, and because this walk often leads me into deep, mystical mind-blizzards, where I am apt to lose all connection with my surroundings, I rely heavily on this sticking quality. I know that when the mist rolls in, my dogs will hear the subtle fog-warnings of my spirit, and pull in closer to make sure that they don't lose me.

At month fifteen, after long daily sessions of specified beggary, I had almost run out of patience. At the same time my list of required canine qualities grew fussier and fussier. I wanted a Lab or a mutt with lots of lab in her, but I didn't want a super young pup, as one typically gets when dealing with a breeder. I was hesitant to adopt a two-month-old that was bound to ruin my life for the first couple of months with sleep deprivation and inappropriate piddling. I've done that three times, which was three times too many. I did, however, wish to raise the dog from a fairly young age because we have so many people coming and going from my husband's recording studio in our back yard, I needed to guarantee that the dog would be friendly to all creatures human. And, although I would have bent a little on this final request, I preferred her to be yellow in hue. This sounds finicky, but the truth is, I have allowed my dogs to lounge around on every piece of furniture and on myself for so many years, that I have adapted all furniture and wardrobe choices to be yellow friendly. Beware entering my house in dark clothes.

I must say here that I never prayed for these fussy specifics without adding a rousing, "But, thy will be done, of course, thy better, smarter, far-seeing will be done!"

There were days when I was tempted to grab the first dog that I saw, days when I would have made a restless choice, a decision inspired by my own notions of proper timing—like the woman who thinks it's time she got married and started a family, and jumps at the first man that crosses her path.

At some point during my search, a friend reminded me of a breeder in the area who raised Labradors. I remembered her name because I had contacted her years earlier, but had never heard back from her. I thought it worth a try to contact her again. This time she did write back telling me that she didn't have any litters planned, and suggested that I periodically check back with her. Given my serious lack of patience, I instantly wrote her off.

One day in May, seventeen months after Tater had taken up residence in the heavens, I sat in my home, holding my lone dog (the one whom I imagined was pining in despair over her empty life), and decided to speak directly, at full-voice volume to the heavens, "Why haven't you sent me a dog?" I asked. "I feel so very ready. What could possibly be the hang up?"

The next morning I got the email. It was the local Labrador breeder whom I had contacted months before. "I have a four month old yellow girl that I have decided not to breed. Are you interested?"

"Yes! Yes! Yes!" I pounded on the keys, "I will be over in two minutes!!"

Her name is Sunshine. She was an instant hit with Cotton and Matt and me, and the cats are being respectful, which is like saying that they are wrapping their paws around her twice daily and covering her head with tender kisses.

Sunshine is often quite calm, (one really can't hope for more), allows me to sleep through the night and practices appropriate toilet habits. She has the deepest pools for eyes, which makes me believe that she will be a profoundly thoughtful adult dog. The timing of her arrival is remarkable, for more reasons than I can number.

She is right. Thank God, she is precisely right.

One of these days I hope to publish a little cookbook with this simple recipe for finding what is best for us:

Take prayer, and mix it with a handful of trust, stir for as long as it takes to mix, which will seem like forever. Add a good deal of patience, and if you don't have any, pray for it. Stir for a good long while, far longer than you have patience for, and, again, if you run out of patience, pray for more. Toss in a little more trust, and if you run out of it, that's right, pray for more. Keep mixing, mixing, mixing... prayer, trust, patience, prayer, trust, patience. Your pantry will come up short on the second and third ingredients almost daily. This is to be expected, don't worry. When you run out, just keep praying, and praying, and praying.

23

Sismano

This past summer my husband and I returned to an area in Italy that we had visited ten years earlier. Umbria is a rural, farming district between the cities of Rome and Florence, more rustic than the much-visited Tuscany, but equally as gorgeous. I went online and found a little bed & breakfast in a medieval hill town that looked like something we might enjoy.

We arrived at the large stone archway of the village, jet-lagged and sleep-deprived, having flown across the great Atlantic overnight and, without pause, hurled ourselves up the wild Italian autostrada. We were ready for the peace of medieval life. Stepping out of our car, prepared to hoof it up to the hotel entrance (these towns rarely allow automobile traffic), we stopped and stared. "We've been here before" Matt said.

"I think you're right," I replied, "but it was so sad, such a neglected old sorry place."

We paused, continuing to soak in the scene.

"Look at it now!" I cooed.

Sismano is a teeny-tiny hill town, as hill towns go. In fact it is really just a castle, a small church, and one stone footpath leading up past fifteen small, connected dwellings, which make a half circle around the castle. All is enclosed within the imposing stone walls of the borgo.

On our previous visit we had stumbled across Sismano while out snooping around the Umbrian countryside. We had pulled into an empty parking area, tiptoed through the great arched stone entrance, so as not to wake the ghosts, and padded up the ancient walkway to the castle entrance. This took all of 45 seconds. We encountered no one, and saw none of the typical signs of Italian life: potted flowers, welcoming benches, sunning cats, friendly faces, spotless attention to front stoop cleanliness. The lack of life was heavy, it choked the place like noxious fumes.

The signs of loneliness were everywhere. If you have ever walked into a long abandoned home you will know what I am attempting to describe. Now imagine this feeling enshrouding an entire village. The absence of love was oppressive, almost chilling, as if the emptiness left behind by the living had invited those from the underworld to move in, and they were throwing a mute weed-and-dust party. We managed the short distance to the castle gate, and then shot back down through the village and out the great arch like fire crackers, determined to shake the dingy mood that clung to our spirits. We erased the name of Sismano from our memories.

Imagine our surprise at finding ourselves once more staring at the great arch of this village.

The scene before us was quite different. The windows sparkled, the old clock ticked, the entrance was a riot of color from the number of potted flowers. One dreamily-scented vine climbed ten feet up the front wall, causing me to wonder whether I had just entered heaven. A small bandstand and dance floor was being constructed in front of the town's entrance. The village looked to be in preparation for some sort of festival. The path up to the castle revealed more and more potted flowers, inviting benches, well-fed cats, tidy, fussed-over doorways.

At the top of the town we were greeted by Ginevra, the owner of the B&B, and her two gentle dogs. She was in her early fifties, very nicely put together (as my mother might have described her), with a welcoming personality. We were given a tour of the B&B, which had clearly been lovingly restored, making use of the small peasant dwellings that surrounded the castle. Our own little house was very comfortable, painted a cheerful yellow, with a small, welcoming fireplace. Ginevra explained that the night we had arrived was the first in twelve of the annual community festa and there would be music and dancing, a different band every night. The village taverna had been taken over by the local women, who had been preparing special dishes for several months. We were encouraged to join in the festivities.

I confess to a low groan when I heard there was going to be a sound system so near my window. I was painfully sleepy and dreaded another night of no rest. It was Wednesday night and it would end early, our hostess assured us.

That evening we squeezed ourselves into the crowded taverna to share the community's home-cooked food with one hundred of our new neighbors eating at long, boisterous tables. Local teenagers handed out homemade gnocchi and roasted pork on paper plates. The food was simple and exquisite. We eventually popped out of the crowded restaurant, and strolled down to the bandstand in front of the village to listen to the music and watch the dancing. The band, composed of an accordion player, a singer and a keyboard player, was tastefully amplified, I was pleased to discover. A drum machine kept a tempo to accompany a two-step dance that looked to be a sort of fox trot. This was mid-week and there were about forty people milling about. Five or six couples danced. They all knew the steps, the very young and the very old, as if each had attended a mandatory two-step class in school. We watched the revelers long enough for me to study each person and attempt to sum up their relationship to those around them, their dominant personality traits, and their relative happiness. I was beginning to worry over some of the seeming wallflowers, those in their forties, sitting with their parents, sitting and sitting, no partners appearing.

The next night we watched the dancers again. There were a few more, perhaps twelve couples on the dance floor at a time, with sixty people sitting around chatting, watching, the same wallflowers sitting in the same spots. I was growing more worried.

The third and final night of our stay we had a cocktail with Ginevra. She explained that Sismano, the castle, the church, the taverna, the peasant dwellings, in short the entire borgo had been owned by her family for close to 800 years, (or was it since the year 800?) A while, at any rate, and after her mother died, the village had fallen into the dreary state that we had found it in ten years earlier. In her mid-forties, after a separation from her husband, Ginevra had decided to move into the old castle and try and revive the ancient place, an extraordinary choice for a modern independently wealthy Italian woman, to give up the comforts of urban life to embrace this faraway place.

Later that evening we visited the festivities. It was Friday night and well over a hundred people were milling about the dance floor, at least thirty couples danced every dance, fathers with babies, ancients with ancients, lovers with lovers, friends with friends. The band was another version of the same make-up as the other nights, with an accordion, keyboard, and this night, a pretty girl singing. I anxiously looked for my wallflowers in their regular seats. They were missing! I worried. It didn't occur to me to look on the dance floor. Finally I saw them, trotting around, changing partners, everyone taking care of their neighbors. I watched a young man with Down's syndrome sitting with his mother. He studied the singer from a seat very near the band, focused, as if waiting for something. Apparently this something arrived, for when a new song was introduced, the young man leapt out of his seat and darted across the dance floor to ask a girl to dance. She accepted and they scooted around the floor, flawlessly weaving in and out of the crowd, as if professionally trained. Everyone danced that evening.

Matt and I stood, watching, enchanted, as if we had stumbled upon a fairy ring in the deep woods. Indeed the contrast between our previous dreary vision of this town and the atmosphere of that evening was so great that it was as if a magic spell had been cast on the town and its surroundings. A love spell.

I started connecting the dots in my head: If Ginevra hadn't loved the old place, if she hadn't opened its doors to the local people and visiting travelers, if the women hadn't cooked the wonderful food, if the band hadn't played to inspire dancing, if the kids hadn't served the guests their meals, if the dancers hadn't come to dance… dot…dot…dot… then the boy wouldn't have had a partner, the lonely wouldn't have found their friends, the old lovers wouldn't have danced with their loved ones and the community wouldn't have broken its cycle of daily isolation. Love seemed that evening to be the answer to all questions.

Love, with its ability to meet any challenge. Love, with its power to breathe life into stone.

24

The Anonymous Ones

There is a tribe of South American Indians, indigenous to the mountains of Columbia, that the Spanish never managed to conquer. They are called the Kogi, and over the years they have traveled farther and farther up into the mountains, where they remain untouched by their Hispanic neighbors. They are secretive and isolated by nature and, until recently, have maintained a policy of unblemished anonymity.

They refer to themselves as the Elder Brothers and consider the people of the industrialized world their younger siblings. Only recently have they broken their silence, in order to warn us that we may be very close to destroying our planet.

They claim to be able to communicate telepathically

with other members of their population, on other, distant mountains, an innate ability that they have been practicing for centuries.

The Kogi's powers of telepathy are most pronounced among their spiritual leaders, wise ones who are carefully singled out early in life and raised to be spiritual guides for the community. These chosen Elders say that there is a council of souls from around the world with whom they regularly consult with their thoughts. And, it is the Kogi, along with this coalition of connected souls, who are hoping to reach out to the Younger brothers (those of us who are busily causing the destruction of our planet) to beg us to turn the situation around.

The Theosophists from the turn of the last century believed in a similar anonymous brotherhood of spirits that was responsible for the progress of love and goodwill for the world. This was a sort of fellowship of adepts, on earth and in the hereafter, who prayed and otherwise aided in the development of the human race.

I am intrigued by this notion, partly because of the romance of it—imagine meeting one of these enlightened souls—but also because of what it implies about our collective thoughts and prayers. It gives hope to those of us who wish to be of use, through prayer, to the advancement of love and harmony for our earthly home.

We spend so much time feeling small and unequal to the task of helping to solve the issues that face us here. We despair of having any effect on the huge problems: wars, world hunger, the poisoning of this beautiful planet. How can our tiny efforts, our miniscule prayers help? At the same time we are embarrassed to pray for our small concerns, our petty wishes, finding it difficult to believe that the great God who watches over all of the planets, the solar systems, the galaxies in the billions would have the time to listen to our tiny domestic concerns.

Today I shamelessly prayed for peace in the Middle East and the return of my missing cat. I do believe that both appeals were heard, and I trust that they are both important to the Great Spirit that watches over this world. "His eye is upon the sparrow," Jesus taught, and I have to believe him.

Maybe we should let God be the judge of the size requirements of an acceptable prayer. Our own ideas are bound to be all out of proportion, and might hinder a worthy prayer from being released and heard.

If we fear we are offering a speck of prayer to knock down an obstacle of mountainous proportions, such as a boiling pot of hatred that looks to be developing into an all out war, we can take comfort in the idea that our prayers are joining those of countless others, to make an anonymous global appeal that might astound us if we could see it. As if all of our prayers were so many doves released into the heavens, and this soaring flock, somewhere in the billions, were flying in perfect formation, creating enormous, gorgeous images of peace for all the world to believe in.

Recently, in my morning meditation in the woods, I have tried to imagine that I am joining a group of concerned, anonymous souls in prayer. I envision them to be both incarnated and in the spirit world, both inside of time and outside it. Our prayers, no matter how simply or grandly expressed, fly off together and are delivered in the most beautiful shapes, extraordinary visions of what the world could look like in perfect peace, in loving harmony with our good mother earth.

I have a fantasy of one day receiving a summons to meet my anonymous prayer alliance. The communication will arrive while I am on my walk in the woods. It might fall from the sky, with its message impressed on the soft side of a leaf. It will direct me to travel to Switzerland or Peru, or somewhere else with an impressive mountain range. My orders will be to board a train on a specific day at a certain time and not to disembark until I have arrived at the final station. I follow my directions carefully, traveling up into the mountains, with the train stopping at increasingly more remote outposts, until it eventually arrives at the second to last station, deep in the hinterlands, and every passenger exits but me. The conductor walks past, and smiles as if he were in on a delicious secret. When I arrive at the station, I step out onto the platform to discover that no one is there (no human, that is), only a profoundly handsome dog, large and thick coated, with a gentle nobility. He watches me with considerable intensity. After several moments, he turns away, turns back to look at me, and then turns again and begins to walk away. I follow him.

He leads me along a gentle path through the mountains, with views of rich, densely wooded valleys on either side. We walk for some time. It is mild summer and exquisitely lovely. Eventually we come upon a view of a delicate round lake surrounded by the most inviting little cabins. I can see small groups of gentle people gathering and talking in soft tones, punctuated by occasional eruptions of joyous laughter. They are waiting for someone, expectant, searching the hills with their eyes. I run down to greet them, all of them strangely familiar but unknown to me on earth. They speak my name as if it were an answered prayer. I will not tell of what we say to each other, it's too private, too sacred, but by the time I depart from this place I am filled with the conviction that the power of our collected prayers can and eventually will make a paradise of this grieving planet.

We would love to have you to join us some day. We gather whenever one of us is praying, so you can't very well miss us. Our numbers shift and change, but we always have just enough to be heard.

25

Noticing

The year I was born, a great-uncle of mine began work on a house on a remote island in the Bahamas. When I was five my mother brought our family there for the first time and since then I have rarely gone a full year without visiting this sweet place. My husband and I have increased our visits since we were married, and I am very grateful that he loves it as much, if not even more fiercely, than I do, connecting us for a lifetime to the island. Its people, its gentle, feminine beauty, violent weather, low, dense, salt-scorched forests, shallow, blind-white sand bars, rich coral reefs, even certain ancient reef fish and resident turtles are old familiars after so many years.

We have shared this place with an army of friends

and family members over the years, but it is always when Matt and I are alone that we have had our most meaningful encounters: sleeping turtles, baby nurse sharks, one rare humpback whale, a strange sighting of what I believed to be a floating Volkswagen bug in the deep waters but which on closer inspection proved to be a whale shark, floating languidly on the ocean surface, his great, gentle head bobbing up and down on the waves.

Dolphin sightings are fairly rare, always the bottlenose variety, and typically traveling in groups of two or three. They will allow our boat to follow them for a few minutes before they lose interest and swim off to hunt. My mother spoke for much of her life of a pair of dolphins she had witnessed once. They had leapt in the air in front of her boat, as if performing for her. She was to mention this experience quite often as she descended into Alzheimer's disease, her hands moving in curves across one another, as if the animals were leaping through a hoop in an act at Sea World. She always had the look of sunshine while relating the story.

On the morning Matt and I had our dolphin encounter, we had just seen the last guest drive off to the airport, and thought it might be a perfect time to go exploring.

The island is surrounded by small cays, tiny islands, many inhabited only by birds and curly-tailed lizards. We thought we'd visit our favorite cay, which was a good half-hour away by boat, and when we arrived we were happy to discover the place empty of visitors.

After a long walk on shore we were wading back out

to the boat when we spotted two dolphins in the distance, perhaps a hundred feet away. We stood chest deep in the water and watched them swim. They kept very close together, caressing each other with their noses and rolling over one another, sometimes lifting their smiling faces, and occasionally their whole bodies out of the water. Matt suggested they might be mating, but I insisted they were only dating, their behavior was so chaste and playful. We stood for some time, studying them, making the sort of nonverbal noises of the awestruck under our breath, not wishing to scare them away.

After a few minutes they came a little closer, and then still closer, always performing their tender movements, until they were so near that if our arms had been just two feet longer we would have brushed them with our fingers, so near we could feel the strong current from their powerful tails as they circled and flipped around us.

Matt and I moved closer to each other, finally grabbing hands. This seemed to bring the dolphins even nearer. It was as if they were attracted to our embrace—when we touched they came within two feet, almost grazing us, but when we lost our connection, they would keep us at more of a distance.

This tendency, by the way, is the opposite of a shark's behavior. Matt once distracted a lemon shark that had been following just a few feet behind my flippers, by taking me under his arm in order to make us look like one big, wide human being. We swam sideways together, watching as the shark lost interest and moved away.

The dolphins, on the other hand, seemed to feel safer

and more curious when we were making ourselves into one person, as if they wished to share in our feeling of union. It felt as though all four of us were joining in the same circle of communion. We spent fifteen minutes together before the gentle pair swam away, leaving us humming with gladness.

LATELY I HAVE been practicing a little ritual on my morning prayer walk. After I release whatever prayers are on my mind, and as I am headed back toward the duties of my day, I hold an imaginary pair of reins in my hands, which guide an imaginary horse, pulling an imaginary cart. I hold these reins with my fingers for a moment and then hand them to my right, as if to the very one to whom I have been praying, adding: "Here, you take over the reins for today. I trust that you will do a much better job than I would."

My next move is to dust my hands off, pick up my head and try and notice the difference. There is a difference, a noticeable difference, or perhaps I should say, I notice differently, with a different quality of attention.

Once, while visiting our island, Matt and I sat on a precipice overlooking a grand panorama of shore and ocean. We sat for a while, quietly drinking in the view, when we looked down to notice a teaming army of ants at our feet. "Look at them," I said, "they have no idea they are in one of the most beautiful spots on earth, no idea of how heavenly this place is."

"Stuck in ant world," Matt replied. We could both relate. But, unlike insects, we have the ability to lift our heads and notice our surroundings.

These days, when Matt and I find ourselves stuck in ant world, one of us will suggest a shift in view. "Let's go for a walk, shall we?" we say. "Let's go for a walk and notice things."

OF COURSE, SOME days are more conducive to noticing than others.

In the Gospel of Thomas, one of the recently discovered gnostic gospels, Jesus is quoted as saying, "*If you do not keep the Sabbath as a Sabbath you will never see the Father.*" The line that precedes this is "*If you do not fast from the world you will not find the Kingdom.*"

Interesting that this rebellious voice, of one who came to shake up the rigid dogma of the Jewish tradition, would be stressing the need for fasting and keeping the Sabbath.

I have been ruminating over this idea of keeping the Sabbath. We live in a culture that has lost sight of the importance of preserving one day a week for laying down the things of the world and focusing on the spiritual. I do not wish to imply that I know how to manage a full day of divine focus, but after reading this line in Thomas's gospel, I thought I would like to at least try.

I chose a recent Sunday to begin.

I had nothing scheduled that day and was alone. This

was helpful, of course. There was no one but me to get in my way, but then I cast a rather large shadow on myself, being so close and all.

I decided to begin the ritual on my daily walk in the woods. This, I thought, would give me a head start, as my walk would count as an hour-and-a-half long mini-Sabbath. The problem is I don't always fast from the world, so to speak, on these walks and waste all sorts of time babbling to myself. But lately, I had been launching a campaign against my inner chatterbox.

I take my morning walk in a neighboring rural park. When I arrive at the parking area, I step out of the car, open the back door where my two dogs are straining to be on their way, snap on their leashes and lead them across a dirt road and onto to a wooded path. After about fifty feet I release the dogs, and send up my first prayer, that they will not scurry back to the parking lot to eat trash. At this point I begin my practice of prayer and contemplation. On most days this practice consists of faint attempts at prayer, interrupted by dashes out to worry over some troublesome thought, followed by a return to feeble prayer, interrupted by a mad foray around the neighborhood to think of ways my neighbors might improve their lives, followed rather contritely by prayers for my neighbors, interrupted by bursts of alarm about some nagging personal worry before I turn back in abject shame to prayer.

In an effort to still this frantic activity, I had recently decided to refrain from any prayers whatsoever on my walk, but to save them for other times during my day. I wished to remain silent and present, allowing my ears to open, eyes to notice, mind to still.

After several days of this practice, for which I must admit, I would have deserved a mark no higher than D minus—I stepped out of my car in the parking lot one morning, and at my feet saw a tiny torn piece of trash from some unrecognizable package, with the words ZIP IT on it.

"Mmm…" I mumbled, pulling an imaginary zipper across my lips.

I came very near getting a B plus that day.

But this is as far as I had gotten with my practice of silence and attention when I tried to keep the Sabbath for an entire day. Like signing up for a triathlon for next Tuesday, it was a tad ambitious.

I began that Sunday morning, as I do every day, pulling into the parking lot and walking my quiet loop through the woods. I didn't grade myself this time, but I didn't anticipate pulling in any awards for contemplation. The difference on this day was that I tried very hard not to dictate what would come next. I was leaving it up to the good angels of the Sabbath.

In short, I noodled. I noodled around the house and at one point thought I might noodle back out for a walk without my madcap dogs. It was spring and there were baby animals out there who were naturally shy around my little terrors. I had just that week noted that I had not yet witnessed my first fawn of the season.

I will never get used to the fact that I live in a place that has such an intimate relationship with the deer. This is an extraordinarily beautiful creature, and I marvel at its loveliness every day. There are those in my neighborhood who see our deer as garden-eating nuisances. I have watched a nursing doe eating fresh roses from off my bushes, and yet still loved her. The rare sighting of one of a deer's newborn is almost more joy than my heart can bear, like a basket of kittens or a hummingbird's nest.

On my appointed Sabbath, in the late morning, I thought I would walk through our neighboring farmland rather than return to the woods. I cut out aimlessly across the fields, always noodling, like a two month old puppy, never traveling in a straight line, stopping to sniff everything, chat with a couple of women on horseback, noodle some more, look at the view, noodle, notice, noodle, sniff, noodle, prick up my ears and stare again, noodle, noodle, inspect a wildflower, noodle, noodle, noodle, sit.

I had only been seated for a few minutes in a little stand of trees at the edge of a field when a fawn, looking to be about three weeks old, tripped by just about fifteen feet from me. This would have been gift enough, had not another tiny newborn fawn popped up from the brush very near me to call to the older one. The tiny fawn nuzzled the older one, and even for a confused moment attempted to nurse from it. If the older fawn could have giggled, he might have sounded a bit like a Disney character. Instead he played and nuzzled and frolicked around the little baby for a few moments, while I sat frozen with ecstatic attention in my place among the trees.

Eventually the older fawn decided to continue on his

way, and the newborn attempted to follow, taking several difficult steps. The older fawn turned to address the tiny one with a parting nod and then sprang effortlessly away, leaving the newborn to sway and stagger back to his nursery very near to me in the woods. He dutifully tucked himself back in his makeshift bed to wait for his mama. I sat with him for a little while longer, drinking him in with my eyes, before deciding it best to make myself scarce so that the mother would not be shy to return.

I walked home as if from a first kiss, dreamy, grateful. "I have seen the Father today," I thought in happy Sabbath wonder, "I have caught a glimpse of the Kingdom."

26

Thank God

When my friends and I gather we often end up talking about our feelings around those we have elected to run our government, and about our current level of involvement, or lack of involvement, in the ups and downs of local, national and international politics. There are days, months, whole years when I have been dragged along by the media as it careened over the violent terrain of political controversy: as we marched off to war, reinstated the practice of torture, tore at the fabric of justice with our prison systems, ignored our poor. During which times my feelings were butted and kicked around like a soccer ball by whoever happened for the moment to have bogarted the biggest microphone. If one has any heart at all, one will care, one must.

Unfortunately, those big microphones are rarely leveled at the mouths of the reasonable, calm, and forward-thinking. Most of the time those instruments are pointed at the minority of aggressive, self-interested blowhards, to whom we wouldn't give the time of day (as the saying goes) in our natural, everyday, non-media-drenched lives.

Then why do we listen?

Perhaps these loud, foolish voices provide some benefits—how else would we learn what thoughts do not resonate, what ideas must not be entertained? But, unless we want to spend our days in repetitive finger-wagging, crying, "Can you believe he said that?!" "Did you hear what she said? Outrageous!" we need to stop and say, "Enough. I've heard enough. I'm off to look for the hopeful voice, for those with creative, curative ideas."

There are certainly red hot buttons in all of us, places, when touched, where we will have a difficult time not reacting. I would never suggest that one shouldn't feel and feel deeply. This would imply that the goal of gathering information is to achieve a state of disinterest. Nonsense. But there comes a point where we must take a deep breath, and try and detach from our stirred-up feelings. There comes a time when we must turn and look for a way through the darkness of today toward a hopeful future.

One of my more sensitive buttons, and I know that I am not at all alone in this, is humanity's shameless treatment of our good, patient Mother Earth. This quite breaks my heart open, and all sorts of anxiety, blame, and fear pours out, doing me and those around me no good. In order to console, some friends will offer the cheerful: "Well, it really isn't the earth that will suffer. She will survive, won't she? It's really only human and animal life that's in jeopardy."

"Gosh," I think. "That hardly relieves the aching."

However glad I might be for the resilience of our brave planet, I have a hunch that it would be more than a tad ungrateful on our part to spoil our deal here. Like being given a scholarship to a beautiful school and drinking beer all day, tossing the cans around the campus and never attending classes. We could very well be expelled, and would roundly deserve it. But, if we are kicked off the planet because of our slovenly and careless conduct, what a rousing shame it would be.

The question is how do we turn this lumbering destructive global attitude around? How do we honor the opportunity to live for our time on planet earth? What can we do to save this beautiful school?

I heard a scientist give a talk in the late eighties from which I have never, thank God, recovered. She was illustrating the point that the traces of household and yard chemicals that we use in the United States were being discovered in colonies of migrating birds in remote islands of the Pacific ocean, where for centuries they had been coming to breed and raise their young. Because of these chemicals, the bird's eggs were no longer able to form into a shell that was hard enough to house a baby bird. The colony was rapidly dying out. She went on to explain that the restrictions on the US's industrial community were much stricter than those on our households, and the effects of this poisoning were reaching all the way around the planet.

The effect of her talk, apart from my racing home and sifting through all of my cleaning and yard products to make sure that they were safe, was to bring home to me how powerful our smallest actions are on all of life. Our tiniest gestures ripple, ripple and continue to ripple constantly, continuously and for all of time. No single action, however diminutive, is lost on the world. If our intention is to care for this good earth, every action we take toward this goal is felt and is ultimately beneficial. We must trust this, and work to find ways of being helpful to our mother planet.

"But," one might say, "you experienced the grace of an enlightening argument for caring for the earth, and not everyone thinks this way. In fact there are seven billion people on the planet presently, and it is probably safe to say that most are not so aware, do not hold the same intention."

This is when I answer, "Well, thank God there is a God, then." Thank God there is a God that is tirelessly watching after our souls, and after our education, who wants nothing more than our enlightenment. And of equal importance, thank God there is a God who is not only intimately involved with our individual spirits but with the spirit of our good Mother Earth. Thank God there is a God who is both intimately involved in our every thought, and universally involved with the health and spirit of this planet.

Thank God there is a God whose hands cradle the world and every soul who has lived and will ever live here.

Do what you can for our precious planet, by all means, and thank God there is a God.

MARGARET DULANEY began writing for the theater while living in New York City in the late-eighties. In the mid-nineties she moved to Bucks County Pennsylvania, where she took up literary nonfiction, (essays exploring divine themes through story and metaphor). She began recording her writings in 2010.

Margaret lives, writes and records from a two-hundred-year-old stone farmhouse and barn, which houses the recording studio, Maggie's Farm. She is married to musician and record producer Matt Balitsaris, founder of the Jazz Record label, Palmetto Records.

She shares her stories every month on her spoken word website Listen Well.

To learn more, please visit:
www.listenwell.org